RECLAIMING COMMUNITY

edited by
Victoria Nash

30-32 Southampton St
London WC2E 7RA
Tel: 020 7470 6100
Fax: 020 7470 6111
postmaster@ippr.org.uk
www.ippr.org
Registered charity 800065

The Institute for Public Policy Research is an independent charity whose purpose is to contribute to public understanding of social, economic and political questions through research, discussion and publication. It was established in 1988 by leading figures in the academic, business and trade-union communities to provide an alternative to the free market think tanks.

IPPR's research agenda reflects the challenges facing Britain and Europe. Current programmes cover the areas of economic and industrial policy, Europe, governmental reform, human rights, defence, social policy, the environment and media issues.

Besides its programme of research and publication, IPPR also provides a forum for political and trade union leaders, academic experts and those from business, finance, government and the media, to meet and discuss issues of common concern.

Production & design by **EMPHASIS**
ISBN 1 86030 134 7
Collection © IPPR 2002
'Community and social exclusion' © M Taylor 2002

Contents

Acknowledgements

IPPR would like to thank Lloyds TSB, Amey, Powergen, BUPA, the Gatsby Charitable Trust, Notting Hill Housing Group and the Peabody Trust for their support. Without their willingness to invest in the Communities Initiative this book would not have been possible. We are also very grateful to Palgrave for allowing us to reproduce material in Chapter 5 which will appear in a forthcoming book *Public Policy in the Community* by Marilyn Taylor.

About the authors

Elizabeth Frazer is Lecturer in the Department of Politics, University of Oxford and Official Fellow in Politics, New College, Oxford. She is the author of *The Problems of Communitarian Politics*, OUP 1999.

Robina Goodlad is Professor of Housing and Urban Studies at the University of Glasgow and was previously founding director of the (Scottish) Tenant Participation Advisory Service. She is co-director of the new Scottish Centre for Research on Social Justice, established in collaboration with Aberdeen University.

Victoria Nash is a Research Fellow at IPPR and is currently directing a programme of research for IPPR's Communities Initiative. She was previously a Lecturer in Politics at Oxford University.

Marilyn Taylor is Professor of Social Policy at the University of Brighton. She has been involved in community development and participation over the past thirty years and has written widely for academic, policy and practice audiences.

Perri 6 is Director of the Policy Programme at the Institute for Applied Health and Social Policy at King's College London. His recent books include *Toward Holistic Governance* and *The Future of Privacy*. He is currently working on a book on social networks and public policy.

Introduction

This book is the interim publication of IPPR's Communities Initiative. This project was established to ascertain how public policy could foster community at the local level in order to improve individual welfare and support key policy aims. The aim of this publication is to identify what it is that a community-sensitive approach to policy-making would add, and to establish some basic principles and definitions that such policy could adopt.

The intuition with which this book begins is that there is indeed something important about the slippery notion of community even if this is not clearly expressed in existing initiatives. Simply put, community matters. The main message carried in these pages is that community-sensitive policy-making and service delivery can improve the character of local social relations for residents and in so doing, help tackle more familiar policy goals such as reducing unemployment, improving health outcomes and minimising social exclusion.

A second theme which runs throughout the book is the importance of reconciling academic and policy debates about community. At the moment there is a significant divide between the two debates, largely focused on disagreement over the meaning and desirability of community. If rebuilding community can in reality improve people's lives then it is vital that these two debates are reconnected, so that policy-makers can gain valuable insight from academic research in this area.

The papers presented in this collection approach these issues from quite different perspectives. As well as offering insight into the value of 'local social networks' and 'social capital', the book discusses ways in which findings from regeneration policy can be extended and applied. As such the recommendations offered and conclusions drawn have important implications for many areas of public policy and also for the design of service delivery. It is hoped that at the very least these chapters will stimulate debate and raise some important questions about the currently under-regarded role of social relations in the pursuit of key policy outcomes.

i

Summary

This book argues that British public policy has neglected to consider the importance of local social relations and their impact on individual welfare and neighbourhood life. The premise from which this book begins is that community matters to individuals and it *should* matter to policy-makers. The various papers that make up this collection approach this idea from different perspectives and, as such, offer a broad range of insights and policy recommendations.

The policy context

It is clearly not the case that public policy fails to take any account of community or social relations. Regeneration initiatives have learnt to address issues of social regeneration as much as physical or economic renewal. Current policy on crime and anti-social behaviour at least recognises the disabling effect of fear of crime on local social interaction and community-building. Debates about active citizenship, civic renewal and public involvement in service delivery all suggest that some thought has been given to the quality of public life and public engagement, whilst the summer 2001 disturbances in Oldham, Bradford and Burnley ensured that 'social cohesion' has appeared as an issue on the political agenda. This is not enough. There is no sense in which we could say that community is a central concern of British public policy. As such, *one of the key aims of this book, and the project from which it stems, is to ensure that the concept of community is mainstreamed*. It is argued that a focus on local social relations would increase the likelihood of current policy aims being achieved. Valued outcomes such as lower levels of crime, improved public health or greater equality of opportunity could all be greatly supported by a policy-making approach that aimed to foster, or at least not harm, positive local social relations. As such, consideration of community should become an integral element of both the policy-making process and the design of public service delivery.

The importance of local social relations

The book's starting point is the observation that local social relations can have a significant effect on individual welfare as well as on the fortunes of an area itself. Even though the relationships we share with others at the local level are unlikely to be the most meaningful or emotionally deep, they can and do make our lives go better in all sorts of important ways. Social relationships are valued most obviously because of how they make us feel: cared for, trusted, liked, comfortable, nervous, scared or depressed. Most of us would probably like to live somewhere where we don't fear our neighbours, where we can at least feel comfortable, even if we want to remain reasonably anonymous. At the next level, local social relationships are important not just for how they feel but because of what they can contribute. Different sorts of relationship can bring support, advice, material help, information and norms or values. At the level above this, local social relationships are valuable because they can have an aggregate effect that benefits all local residents. For example, neighbourhoods where residents are generally responsible and trusting of each other are likely to be areas with lower crime rates and a well-maintained public environment.

These are the reasons why a focus on local social relations is important: if positive local relations are fostered they will both improve individual welfare and help ensure the achievement of important policy goals. This is a point which regeneration policy has taken to heart. This inter-relationship does not seem to have been embraced in other policy areas, however, with the result that few initiatives seem to take account of their effect on local social networks or behaviour. This appears to be the case even when initiatives could achieve their aims more effectively by taking the contributions of social networks into account.

One thing that it is important to note is that although local social relations can contribute greatly to both individual well-being and policy goals, it is not enough to focus on social relations alone. Although recent debates about 'social capital' may have made it sound as if this is some marvellous cure-all, it is quite clear that improving the quality of local social relations will not by itself improve economic prosperity or raise educational standards. It may be true that social capital is a necessary condition of our achieving most key policy outcomes but it certainly cannot be a sufficient one.

Community as a policy goal

One of the reasons why policy has neglected the import of local social relations (and social relations more generally) is no doubt the complexity of the subject matter. This is an issue on which there is little crossover between academic and policy debates. It is probably true that we have far less understanding of the impact of policy on social relations than we do of its economic consequences. It is for this reason that the collection starts from the point of community. This is a term which already has policy resonance and which means something to all of us. The difficulty comes in trying to pin down in what sense community is important and to what extent it can stand as an appropriate policy goal. One purpose of this collection is to unravel the overlap between academic studies of community and social relations, policy discourse and aims, and our everyday understanding of the benefit that community brings. The challenge is to articulate exactly what it is that we gain from enjoying certain sorts of social relations at the local level and to find ways of supporting, or at least not undermining this, through policy initiatives.

Community is a difficult word. We may think we know what it means but it is notoriously hard to pin down. Both political theory and sociology regard the term with some ambivalence, whilst, as some of the contributions note, many of the concerns about community reflect reasonable fears that certain types of community will prove to be intolerant or exclusionary. All this controversy contrasts sharply with our common-sense, everyday interpretation of community which sees it as an unproblematically good thing. A *second aim of this book is therefore to ensure that we face up to the challenges of academic rigour, and that 'community' can be seen as a respectable policy concern*. This means accepting that when we refer to community we are describing an explicitly normative state of affairs: to state that policy should support or foster community means that policy should support or foster a particular type of local social relations.

It is clearly not the case that one particular model of social relations can 'fit all'. In an ideal world it would be desirable for policy-makers and service deliverers to have a precise understanding of the social implications of all their decisions. In the absence of such a possibility it is useful to have a shorthand account of the sort of social relations each area should manifest. This would enable policy decisions to take into account likely social effects of a policy without having to draft in a sociologist or social theorist. The idea of community can provide such a shorthand if it is appropriately defined.

It is very important not to over-romanticise the notion of community, and all the contributions in this collection carefully avoid doing so. Traditionally this word has evoked ideas of closely-tied and solidaristic social relations. Now it is not clear that this is an image of neighbourhood relations that any of us would aspire to, or indeed one which could provide us with the full range of valuable benefits we could hope to receive. In this light all chapters stress the importance of having neighbourhoods that are characterised by multiple, overlapping social ties, with a mixture of the strong ties that bind to us to others like ourselves, and the weak ties that connect us casually with groups different to ourselves.

Although a loose definition of community is proposed in Chapter 1, each contribution takes a slightly different perspective. As such the views presented are intended to raise some discussion about issues of community in public policy, revealing a wide range of policy implications without imposing a particular blueprint. Each chapter makes clear the different ways in which a policy-making approach that is sensitive to community or social relations can have significant implications for individual welfare and key policy goals.

Chapter summary

The book is structured in three parts, organised around the following questions:

- Why does community matter?

- What could a community-sensitive approach add to policy-making?

- How do existing policies measure up?

Chapter 1 aims to set out some basic principles and definitions which make it clear why community could have an impact on individual welfare and policy outcomes. It is first of all explained why we cannot assume that existing 'community' initiatives necessarily focus on 'community' in the same sense that the book does. It is suggested that existing initiatives use the word 'community' in three different ways, only one of which actually adds anything of interest:

- Community as an *agent*, as in the community involvement element of Local Strategic Partnerships, which really just refers to the group of residents who will be involved.

- Community as a *place*, as in the New Deal for Communities, where community seems to mean the same as 'neighbourhood'.

- Community as a *value*, as in the National Strategy for Neighbourhood Renewal's focus on 'reviving communities', where the focus is not just a groups of people or place, but on rebuilding certain valued sets of social relations.

It is the third of these senses which is the focus of this book. A two-stage argument is made, showing first of all why policy should value certain types of social relations, and secondly, why a subset of those relations which can be called local 'community' might be of particular value. It seems that there are at least three levels at which local relationships are important from a policy perspective. Most obviously, the quality of local social relations affect the quality of life of individuals and families. It is simply not pleasant to live in an area where you either fear or do not trust your neighbours. More indirectly, the different relationships we are immersed in at local level may be important for providing certain goods or benefits such as baby-sitting services, information about jobs or plumbers, or even personal support. At the aggregate level, there is evidence to show that areas with a predominance of certain types of social relations or *social capital*, will be healthier, more prosperous or less crime-ridden than others.

Local social relations affect individual welfare or behaviour in three different ways which can give rise to the sort of benefits outlined above:

- Social capital or social network effects: who you know and how well you know them matters.

- Socialisation effects: the social environment in which we live or grow up can exert subconscious pressure on our values, expectations and perceptions.

- Attachment effects: the effects of attachment to place or a sense of belonging can have an important impact both on individual well-being and on consequent behaviour.

Although it is easy to make a convincing case as to why local social relations matter, it is slightly more difficult to justify why policy need be concerned with 'community' strictly speaking. This term is one which academic literature treats with some distrust, largely because it often invokes ideas of similarity, exclusivity or intolerance. The definition of community that is proposed in this chapter is very different and explicitly accepts that if policy is to promote community it must only promote relations that are inclusive and civil. As such an appropriate definition of community would be:

> Social relations of a trusting and civil nature, where those relations are grounded in a shared commitment to the neighbourhood or area.

This definition seems to capture both the essence of many policy debates about the importance of 'community' whilst still recognising the potentially sinister side of this ideal. Further to this, and in the light of the different types of benefit of different types of social relations we might add that *each local area should display a mix of different sort of social groups and ties.*

Chapter 1 ends by suggesting that policy needs to take account of community at three different levels.

- At the broadest level, a concern for community must be mainstreamed so that all major policy decisions have some consideration for community effects.

- At the next level, particular policy goals such as crime reduction require especially careful attention to the ways in which more positive social relations can be supported.

- At the most specific level, different initiatives may target particular neighbourhoods or areas which have experienced community breakdown.

Chapter 2 and Chapter 3 together answer the question of what sort of benefit could be expected from a community-sensitive approach to policy-making. Chapter 2 develops the idea that social networks carry important goods that are of value to individual well-being, and asks what those networks can deliver, and in what circumstances government could intervene to shape those networks. The realm of 'friendship and acquaintance' is after all, one which has traditionally been thought to be beyond the legitimate reach of the state.

There is certainly a great deal of academic evidence which links certain key policy outcomes with particular patterns of social network ties. Arguing that social capital is too blunt a tool to capture the detail of what it is that individuals gain (or lose) from different types of social relationship, Perri 6 suggests that policy needs to develop a more network-sensitive approach. In particular he argues against the idea that 'all good things go together' and suggests that in some circumstances the sorts of social ties that provide an individual with say, employment contacts, may not be the sort of ties that can also provide emotional support in times of need. Similarly, there may be a conflict between the strong ties of engagement and commitment required to turn around a slipping area and the weaker, more casual ties required to connect individual residents of that area with more affluent or powerful groups outside.

These 'networks conflicts' do not mean that policy-makers should avoid affecting personal social networks of 'friendship and acquaintance'. It is extremely unlikely that they could do so if they tried. Public policy affects the shape and character of social networks unavoidably – just as housing policy affects who lives next to whom, so transport or education policy affects the extent to which different social groups can or cannot intermingle. These are just some of the most obvious ways in which policy has an unavoidable effect. Building on this claim, Chapter 2 argues that it is no better for government to influence people's social relationships unintentionally than to do so deliberately but carefully. It is also the case that government does possess various types of policy tool which could be used to limit network harm or even encourage the development of new valuable social ties.

In order to illustrate this claim, Perri 6 picks two policy areas where a more network-sensitive approach could further stated policy aims. The Employment Gateway of the New Deal for example, is criticised for taking insufficient account of an individual's informal ties, the development of which may eventually prove valuable in finding employment. As well as offering precise recommendations for the service itself, some wider recommendations for increasing social interaction between groups at the local level are offered:

- Transport planning should prioritise the connection of low income estates to more affluent areas.

- Land use planning should focus more on supporting residential communities with a variety of leisure and other facilities that support interaction and mixing.

- Support to young people in care should focus on reducing social isolation and encourage the formation of a broad range of social ties.

If the main contribution of Chapter 2 is to emphasise the importance of local social networks and their impact on key policy outcomes, Chapter 3 adds a new dimension to the argument by looking at the value of certain local goods that support community. The argument is that community might matter not just for the social relationships it supports but also for the value of what has to be shared at the local level. Community assumes that some common interest in, or attachment to the locality is shared by residents, and in order for this to be the case there has to be some degree of genuinely shared 'public' life at the local level. The suggestion is that public policy currently takes insufficient account of how genuinely public and shared local goods can be maintained, or indeed why this might be important.

Elizabeth Frazer examines the case for suggesting that two important types of good should be genuinely shared and communal in a neighbourhood or locality. Public spaces, clean, safe streets and local amenities are one such good. This is just as much because of the symbolic importance of such spaces in supporting a 'public realm' where citizenship can be lived out and where different groups can intermingle, as because of the practical difficulties of living in a world where there is only private land. The second type of political good which needs to be shared at the neighbourhood level is values, modes of conduct and ways of life. This doesn't mean that everybody has to have the same moral values or systems of belief – quite the opposite – in a diverse society it is important to recognise the 'differences between us' as well as emphasising 'the things we all share'. It is simply that without some minimally shared standards of 'civil' behaviour or acceptable conduct, neighbourhoods can quickly become uncomfortable and fearful places to live. Public policy may often shy away from discussing this matter, but norms, values and ways of life are a key political issue in modern societies with all their problems of social fragmentation and exclusion.

In many of our urban neighbourhoods both these shared goods have broken down (land is neglected, street furniture vandalised and walls graffitied). Anti-social behaviour can mean that people become scared to leave their homes. One way of thinking about this decay is to cast it as a 'tragedy of the commons', whereby goods become hard to preserve principally because they are shared and seemingly no one person's responsibility.

Elizabeth Frazer uses this argument to think through how policy-makers could respond to urban decay or community breakdown. Her analysis shows that often the solutions to this problem fail to take into account any consideration of what is required for a good to be genuinely shared and public within any one area. Parks or streets may be effectively 'privatised' by the introduction of private security or the domination of particular social groups. The facilities or amenities provided cannot be genuinely public unless some effort is made to address the needs of 'disorganised' dynamic groups as well as more stable and easily visible interest groups. Location of these amenities matters as well: policy tends to project a particular 'shape' onto a neighbourhood without thinking whether this reflects the 'map' that local residents might draw. Frazer also suggests that there is a tendency to see neighbourhoods as 'enclaves' where all facilities should be focused on the centre. A preferable model would be to place some amenities on the periphery of areas in order to ensure a flow of people across different localities. In order for public life to be genuinely shared not just within neighbourhoods but across society, such spaces and facilities should be used to ensure that neighbourhood boundaries are permeable and overlapping rather than rigid and enclosing.

Chapters 4 and 5 identify the lessons that can be learnt from existing 'community-focused' policy. British regeneration policy is the only public policy area to take community seriously, even if there are still serious inadequacies in its approach. Chapter 4 looks at current successes, and asks whether or not our experience of community participation in regeneration has taught us any lessons about building community that could be applied to other policy areas. Although as noted above the phrase 'community involvement' means no more than 'involving local residents' it is possible that such a process can genuinely build community by giving residents a greater sense of investment in their area and by helping to build bonds between groups or individuals on this basis.

Drawing on English and Scottish regeneration policy, Robina Goodlad makes several recommendations which have clear relevance for other policy areas. Her first point is that attention to community is unavoidable: if people think that social relations matter, then it is impossible to have democratic governance without some reference to community. Equally it is impossible to judge the impact of any policy initiative without taking account of community, because that impact will depend on the character of social relations existing in specific places at any one time.

Experience of community participation in regeneration and renewal allows us to develop guidelines which can ensure that, whatever the policy area, such participation helps to foster community. This chapter argues that it is essential not to assume homogeneity of community identity; just because we talk of 'community involvement' as if it just meant involving something we call 'the community' does not mean that the sociological reality will match this. Most areas will manifest a variety of different groups and interests which all have to be considered. It is also important to recognise that fostering community can be both a means as well as an end in its own right. Other important goals can be furthered by improving the character of local social relations as this summary has made clear. But it is vital that residents' aspirations are considered in this light as well as policy-makers, or the confidence of residents in officials will be undermined. There are also clear signs that structure and design of participation methods make a great deal of difference to the quality of the outcomes, but in this respect the most important factor is that participating residents feel a sense of efficacy. It need not be the case that participants achieve everything they ask for, but residents must gain a perception that they have been listened to or taken seriously. Without such a sense of efficacy, disillusionment will be quick and community may be undermined rather than fostered.

Perhaps the most radical suggestion, and certainly the one which has the most far-reaching implications is the suggestion that capacity-building should apply to public officials as well as residents. Although housing and regeneration officials have most experience of building participation structures, other public officials need to be trained in such a way that they come to see how they could and should foster community at the local level. This might mean sharing experience and skills between officials from different policy backgrounds.

Chapter 5 asks not just about policy successes but about policy failures. Marilyn Taylor revisits the language of community, social capital and civil society and asks why it has recently achieved so much credence. The suggestion is that 'community' and associated terms are seen as offering an alternative approach to several key policy concerns such as the breakdown of moral cohesion and responsibility, and the breakdown of democracy or political legitimacy. The most prevalent use of this language comes with attempts to reduce social exclusion and rebuild slipping neighbourhoods.

In this context, Chapter 5 suggests that the language of community can be damaging where it encourages an over-simplification of complex issues. The term itself as stated earlier, has important limitations, and any policy use must explicitly reject the more exclusionary implications. If this were merely a matter of linguistics then little damage would be caused. The danger comes when talk of 'rebuilding community' in poor neighbourhoods results in measures to develop social relations that are inappropriate to the area. In particular, Taylor rejects the idea that there is 'less community' in deprived neighbourhoods if this means strong, solidaristic social ties. Research shows that many residents are often well-integrated within the area. What such residents may lack, though, are casual 'weak ties' to people different from themselves beyond the neighbourhood. Thus, community policies need to focus on the development of weaker social ties or 'bridging' social capital, and these ties should not be based just on employment but should range across as wide a range of activities and areas as possible.

There is also a concern that residents in poor areas may be called upon to manage their own exclusion. It is all very well focusing on rebuilding community, but unless this is matched by a commitment from public agencies to maintain local services and invest time, money and effort in the area, the sense of isolation will remain. This also means that problems of low staff morale have to be addressed especially amongst those operating at the frontline who have much contact with local residents. Issues of trust also arise in relation to the current vogue for partnership working. There has to be more flexibility in the timing and structure of partnership work. It takes time to build trust, and this may often be undermined by the bureaucratic processes of appraisal, monitoring and audit. As well as focusing on the role of agencies it is vital that more attention is paid to the role of social entrepreneurs or community leaders. In particular policy needs to consider the ways in which community leaders can remain embedded in the communities they represent, and how both accountability and succession can be achieved.

Chapter 5 concludes by making several recommendations to ensure that the strengths of community discourse are harnessed and its pitfalls avoided. The most fundamental requirement is that policy and practice should be based in a strong foundation of community and network development. This means working to build sustainable overlapping networks of various kinds at the local level, as well as encouraging events that make networks visible, reinforce local links and give people a common sense of identity. It is also essential that policy recognise the importance of weak ties and thus that it should support the development of multiple, overlapping networks that offer people choices and opportunities beyond their locality.

None of this is possible without a deeper understanding of community engagement, which can avoid romanticising local social relations to appreciate how local people engage with each other and the outside world in different political and economic circumstances. This is the primary challenge that community-aware policy-making must face, and which is an apt conclusion to all the preceding chapters.

I: Making the case for community

1. Why community matters

Victoria Nash

This book starts from the premise that community matters to individuals and, as such, that it should matter in public policy. The argument presented throughout is that local social relations have a significant impact upon individuals' quality of life. This impact stems both from the personal satisfaction or distress that results from certain sorts of social relations as well as from the more indirect benefits or harms that certain relationships can bring. Despite the current recognition that social regeneration is as important as physical or economic renewal in turning an area around, there has been a general neglect of social relations in British policy-making. In an ideal world, policy-making would take full account of the subtle effects of different social networks or norms in every policy judgement. Given the impracticality of this ideal it is suggested here that a preferable alternative is to use the idea of 'community' as a suitable guide. If we can identify a broad model of the sorts of social relations that every area or neighbourhood should enjoy, then it should be possible to ensure that public policy works to support such types of relation rather than undermine them.

This introductory chapter lays out some basic principles and arguments that support the more sophisticated analysis of the rest of the book. As well as setting out some of the basic ways in which local social relations affect individual welfare, it is important to clear the ground by first addressing the rhetorical baggage that 'community' traditionally comes with. Although 'community' is a word that evokes no amount of good things, the sense in which we will suggest it can constitute a suitable concern or goal for public policy must be unambiguous and rhetoric-free. If, as some cynics suggest, the term 'community' is most frequently used in situations where its emotive overtones cover up existing divisions and difficulties, then we have a challenge on our hands. Is community a suitable goal or focus for public policy, and if it is, what makes it so?

As well as trying to show why the idea of community needs careful handling, this chapter will also outline the range of benefits that a community-sensitive approach to policy-making and service delivery might produce. Some attempt will be made along the way to show how 'community' can fit in with other related terms such as social capital and social networks.

Defining community for public policy ends

Although community may sound like an unproblematically good thing, it is actually a very difficult idea. As well as being used in a variety of different senses in everyday speech, often with emotive effect, academic literature has traditionally fought over the extent to which community is cosy and appealing or sinister and exclusionary. As it stands there is certainly little agreement as to what type of social relations are captured by 'community'. If we want to treat community as a policy goal then the first thing we must do is clarify exactly what we mean by that term. That process of clarification is challenging for the following reasons:

- *The term 'community' is used by different people in different ways.* At least three very different types of use can be identified: community as a simple description or collective noun, describing a group of people who share some common factor such as a trade; community as a value, describing the normative ideal whereby a neighbourhood or place is characterised by close ties and solidarity between residents; and community as an action, whereby a community is seen as an agent looking to change its own circumstances (Glen 1993).

- *There is little crossover between debates about community in academic literature and its use in public policy.* The word community is used loosely and without rigour in policy debates, either as a synonym for neighbourhood, or as a warm, rhetoric-laden but fairly meaningless term. Academic debates about the term often focus on the difficulty of arriving at a single definition of community, or its possibly negative connotations, and consequently fail to recognise its appeal as a policy-making goal.

- *Within academic debates, and specifically within political theory, community is interpreted in a variety of ideological ways*, ranging from the nostalgic or moralising views of communitarians on the right to the solidaristic, liberating notions of traditional socialism on the left. To complicate matters further, the so-called 'liberal-communitarian' debate has falsely contrasted individual well-being with collective well-being, such that community-focused policies tend to be seen as necessarily threatening to personal rights.

The overall effect of these disagreements is to confuse policy debates about community almost irredeemably. As Peter Wilmott commented in his study of community initiatives, 'At times, the multiplicity and variety of applications seems so diverse as to render the term almost meaningless' (Wilmott, 1989). The accuracy of this observation is clear when we reflect that even within the current range of community-focused policy initiatives the term is used in several very different ways. Consider:

- Community as an agent, as in the community involvement element of Local Strategic Partnerships.

- Community as the target or place of action, as in the New Deal for Communities (where it often seems to just mean 'a neighbourhood').

- Community as a value, as in the National Strategy for Neighbourhood Renewal's focus on 'reviving communities'.

This diversity of uses means that defending the statement 'community matters' is difficult. In what sense does community matter? Any one definition of community that is chosen will in some sense always be arbitrary as it means ignoring lots of other possible definitions. Just as we don't shy away from trying to produce socially just policies simply because there are many different interpretations of justice (not all of which we agree with), so we shouldn't shy away from pursuing community as a policy goal as long as we're prepared to state what we think it stands for. Specifically we are trying to identify the sense in which community matters to individuals and families and therefore should matter to policy-makers or service deliverers. The challenge is to arrive at an understanding of community that captures what is generally felt to be valuable about community whilst balancing this with a need for rigour and clarity. It is also essential to recognise the potential pitfalls of community. Many of the negative aspects of 'community' that are raised in academic debates actually reflect real fears about the darker side of certain sorts of community, namely that although close and supportive, they might be intolerant, exclusionary or backward-looking. Thus when we recommend to policy-makers that they support and foster community, we must be prepared to offer an explicitly normative definition of what we mean by 'community'. Not all types of community can or should be supported by government.

The first step towards understanding why community matters in public policy is to think a bit more carefully about how the term is used and which uses seem to capture something valuable. In many policy statements and initiatives, 'the community' is used interchangeably with 'neighbourhood', the assumption being that both refer to groups of people in an area. Used in this sense, 'community' adds nothing new to policy-making. In other uses, as in 'community involvement' or 'community capacity-building', the term really just refers to local residents, and again adds little of interest. In some uses, however, (as with the SEU's references to 'reviving communities'), 'community' seems to mean more than just an identifiable group of people, it describes some sort of social relations between them. In this sense, 'community' does mean something more than just 'neighbourhood' or 'locale'.

This is a good starting point. It suggests a new way for government to think about its impact on citizens. The most enduring focus of British governments has been on individuals and households: poverty, for example was seen as appropriately dealt with by doling out benefits based on either individual or household incomes. Area-based initiatives have also waxed and waned in popularity, but have always been grounded in the recognition that local factors such as the regional or local economic context can have a significant impact on individual opportunity structures. The heightened focus on neighbourhoods since 1997 (formalised by the establishment of the Social Exclusion Unit and Neighbourhood Renewal Unit) stems from the further recognition that deprivation can be compounded within a very small area as different factors unite to create a vicious circle of spiralling decay. As we have seen above, however, 'community' implies something more, namely that policy should be concerned not just with individuals and households, or indeed the geography of poverty, but should instead attend to the relations between those individuals or within that area.

So what exactly will this focus on social relations bring to public policy? And can we justify the move from the focus on 'social relations' to a concern with 'community'? As stated above, 'community' is often interpreted as a value-laden term, implying a certain sort of social relation between people, and those social relations may not be ones that we think are appropriate to be fostered (or interfered with at all) by government. Should policy-makers or service deliverers have any concern whatsoever with our social relationships? Surely these are private and beyond the bounds of legitimate state interference? Whilst Perri 6's paper will give a more thorough response to this question, the following section will consider some of the reasons why having a concern for local social relations might seem like a reasonable idea.

Why public policy should be concerned with local social relations

The presumption so far has been that community is to do with place. As a stand-in for 'neighbourhood' or as a way of referring to the social relations that go on in that neighbourhood, the assumption has been that community either describes a place or the social relations occurring within that area. There is an alternative however. Community of interest can also be of relevance to public policy. The Neighbourhood Renewal Action Plan for example, refers explicitly to the role that faith groups can play in local strategic partnerships even when they straddle neighbourhood boundaries (SEU 2001:52). For many of us, communities of interest and other non place-based communities such as family networks, old school friends, or fellow members of church provide more supportive social relationships than our immediate circle of neighbours. In this sense dwelling on 'community of place' and the importance of local social relations could seem at best just irrelevant and at worst a waste of resources.

In fact, as should be made quite clear in the following chapters, there is no need to assume that community of place is more important than community of interest, or that our closest social relationships do occur at the level of the neighbourhood. (Indeed there is good reason to hope that this will not always be the case, as Marilyn Taylor's paper emphasises.) Furthermore, it is perfectly possible to accept this point and still believe that community of place and local social relations matter. It just means acknowledging that different sorts of relationships are valued for different policy reasons. The relationships we find ourselves emmeshed in at the residential level are important not because they will necessarily provide us with emotional support, financial aid or companionship (they might), but because they can provide lots of other things we value, for example, a sense of belonging, a feeling of trust or access to goods such as baby-sitting, car-sharing or a clean environment.

In line with the current government emphasis on quality of life at the local level, there is therefore good reason to focus on community of place. Perhaps even more importantly, there is some concern that it is precisely the break-down of these local social relationships that makes delivery of policy goals such as clean, safe streets or positive public health outcomes harder to accomplish. In this sense, we might just think that it matters what sort of relations people share within a neighbourhood, both because those relations could matter to individuals themselves and also because the nature of those relations impacts on public goods such as service delivery, crime levels, or physical quality of the living environment. On this point, there is increasing, but still insufficient, recognition that public services cannot be improved through economic investment alone, but need some form of social investment. It is probably also true to say that the effect of policies such as those concerning housing, transport, planning, education or policing will impact far more heavily on area-based social relations than on relations of kin, faith or other interests.[1]

Community of interest should be acknowledged to play an important role in providing social support and friendship, and it is essential that we are aware of the ways in which interest-based community groups can interact with community of place. The importance of this is highlighted by the events that took place in the summer of 2001 in Bradford, Burnley and Oldham where tensions between communities of interest were heightened, among other things, by regeneration funding measures which pitted local areas against each other in the competition for funding.

Having stated the broad reasons why community of place might matter in contrast to community of interest, it is worth spelling out some of the arguments in more detail. It was stated above that community of place can deliver important goods both for individuals and the state. The high profile of Robert Putnam's work has ensured that the concept of *social capital* is now a relatively familiar one. It captures the idea that social relationships are themselves a resource. As Putnam puts it: 'Just as a screwdriver (physical capital) or a college education (human capital) can increase productivity (both individual and collective), so too social contacts affect the productivity of individuals and groups' (Putnam 2001). This makes perfect sense if we think of the way in which trust helps to smooth co-operative efforts, or the way in which a local organisation with good political contacts can more easily achieve its aims. Some of the most oft-praised physical regeneration projects such as those run by the Groundwork charity have proved successful precisely because they have focused on ways of building trust between local residents in the process.

The most frequently quoted (but rather complicated) definition of social capital is 'features of social organisation such as networks, norms and social trust that facilitate co-ordination and collaboration for mutual benefit' (Putnam, 1995). The most productive groups will be those where there are many social connections and high levels of trust, quite simply because this is what will smooth the flow of information or make co-operative activity easiest. This makes sense if we look at two aspects of our relationships with others that we would never usually consider:

- Firstly, the structure of social relationships such as how close they are or how well we know the other person, affects what the relationship will help to provide. Money in the form of friendly loans, for example is unlikely to change hands except within close relationships such as family or friendship-based networks. Information or gossip, on the other hand, will spread most quickly and effectively across networks of people who know each other on a more casual basis, the whole point of gossip being the relating of facts to groups who don't already know about them.

- The second component of social capital is the norms that govern relationships which clearly affect the type of interaction that can result. The most valuable norm is of course social trust which makes co-operation possible and safe, that reduces the fear of crime, and maybe even affects our relationship with government. Other relevant norms are reciprocity, common habits of engagement or common signs or meanings which make co-operation predictable and easy. Even body language such as eye contact, or shaking hands are remarkably important elements of the process of getting along with others.[2]

Quite why social capital is a valuable resource can best be seen in the range of recent research examining the relationship between high levels of social capital and various desirable policy outcomes. Studies have shown correlations between social capital and health (Kawachi *et al*, 1997), lower crime rates (Halpern, 1999, Putnam, 2001), educational achievement (Coleman, 1988) and improved economic performance (Fukuyama, 1995). Putnam's own seminal work suggested a correlation between levels of social capital and the efficacy of local government (Putnam, 1995). In each case the various research studies focus on the different types of positive effect that social relationships can offer. In the case of local government for example, Putnam's own research suggests that higher levels of civic participation in anything from choirs to bowling leagues encourage greater levels of social trust and a more horizontally-ordered society. This inhibits the development of the culture of secrecy and nepotism required for corrupt local government. In the case of lower crime levels the suggestion is that local social norms (social trust versus self-interest) and willingness to take responsibility and intervene are associated with this outcome. Although this may just sound like stating the blindingly obvious, this should just make us more suprised that so little account is currently taken of the effect of policy on local social relations.

Most of these arguments about the benefits of social capital usually present it as a 'public good'. If you live in an area where people are generally trusting then you will reap some of the benefits (such as easy credit arrangements, willingness to lend and share goods, for example) whether you are a trusting person yourself or not. In this sense many of these authors would say that it is just a good thing for an area to display a higher level of social capital, where that means higher levels of social trust, well-understood norms of behaviour and reasonable levels of social interaction. On this view, one of the reasons why local community matters is because of the supply of social capital it can generate for all residents, and the various policy goals which that might help to achieve.

Some researchers see social capital as too blunt an instrument to capture what it is about different types of social relations that is important. In particular, they regard the claim that social capital is a public good delivering a wide range of benefits to all as just too sweeping a claim. Sociologists who study what they call *social networks* look very carefully at the different types of social relationship which individuals enjoy and determine whether these relationships provide the sort of goods that those individuals personally need. If we compare the needs of say a young unemployed person with those of a widowed pensioner, we can see that each would benefit from a different type of social ties. When you are looking for a job, it is helpful to have lots of contacts to different types of people, so that you can access as much information about possible opportunities as possible. This means you need lots of 'weak' or 'bridging' social ties which are casual relationships with people unlike yourself that connect you to different groups. A widowed pensioner on the other hand may need a lot of social support, and in particular emotional support. This is hard to get from casual acquaintances and is only really forthcoming from 'strong' or 'bonding' ties to family and friends (people similar to yourself). The argument is, then, that a blunt 'social capital' approach will take insufficient account of personal network needs and benefits.

On this view then, one of the things we might want from our local area is a mix of different sorts of social contact. Without knowing about specific individual needs and contacts we cannot say what sort of social ties are most important in a particular neighbourhood. (Although as the last two chapters will show, social exclusion in deprived areas is often characterised by a lack of weak ties to different groups outside the area.) What we can suggest is that all will benefit if there are multiple overlapping different social groups living locally, with plenty of opportunities for local social interaction. In this way, there will be opportunities for individuals to build the sorts of social ties that they specifically will benefit from. This social networks argument is a more subtle version of the social capital argument.[3] It suggests that one of the reasons why policy-makers should be concerned with local social relations is because it can help them avoid damaging local social networks that contribute in very important ways to individual welfare.

So far discussion has focused on what it is that social relationships can provide. These arguments do not assume that the relationships experienced are necessarily local. In fact, as earlier mention of 'communities of interest' suggested, people may get most of their social support, values or identity from groups that extend beyond the area where they live. In other words, social networks or social capital need not have a local geographic base. One of Putnam's own claims, in fact, is that we are investing fewer and fewer resources in the places where we live. If this is the case, why should we dwell on community of place, on building relationships of trust and civility at the neighbourhood level?

The answer is that local social relationships do matter for three important reasons. The first of these has really been referred to above – research such as that on crime does show that it is precisely the quality and structure of local social relationships which can have an effect on an area's crime figures. We might expect the same to apply for outcomes such as lower levels of vandalism or well-maintained local public spaces. It is just common sense that the most effective way of achieving these outcomes would be to raise levels of social responsibility or trust amongst residents living in the area, so that they don't act in an anti-social manner and may even step in if they see other pople doing so. This approach is very much about looking at the causes of crime and trying to change the behaviour patterns that can cause it. In cases such as these then, it would seem that social capital does genuinely have to be local in order for it to have the required local effect.

The second reason why policy-makers should be concerned with specifically local social relations is to do with the impact of our social environment on our identity, values and expectations. As a recent Joseph Rowntree study noted, our local social networks 'are more than simply routes to opportunities and material resources. The nature and quality of these networks affect how we see ourselves and others, the values we hold and the general quality of lives we lead.' (Forrest and Kearns 1999). The National Strategy for Neighbourhood Renewal consultation document also noted that as deprived neighbourhoods become increasingly cut off from surrounding areas, young people are particularly affected as they can come to grow up with 'a narrow view of life and few positive role models' (SEU, 2000a). These comments on the effects of our neighbourhood experiences highlight the importance of one particular process – socialisation. Who we are, how we see ourselves and the world, what we expect from life – all of these perspectives can be shaped by our relationships with the people we live amongst. This may matter most in poor areas. It is quite likely that young people growing up in deprived neighbourhoods are disproportionately affected by their peer group relationships simply because they have less occasion to experience anything else.

As well as affecting our aspirations and expectations local social relations can also shape our values, our behaviour patterns and our self-respect. PAT 8 identifies the various risk factors associated with the development of anti-social behaviour. Among those factors are parental criminality and peer-group involvement in problem behaviour (SEU, 2000b). One of the reasons why recent housing policy has actively tried to promote principles of mixed tenure is to avoid concentrations of low income families on single estates which can provide children with only a very limited set of role models. Research in social psychology also shows that contact with different groups during childhood and adolescence may significantly affect whether people grow up with very stereotyped views of members of other social and ethnic groups (Miller and Brewer, 1984; Hogg and Abrams, 1988). If we are genuinely trying to work towards a discrimination-free society then government must attend to the detail of local social relations and their effect on our views, a point which the recent Denham and Cantle reports into the 2001 summer disturbances have highlighted but which still need significantly more attention (Home Office, 2001a; Home Office, 2001b).

On the issue of how we come to see ourselves and how others see us, some studies have highlighted the devastating extent of ostracisation or stigmatisation that some residents may undergo simply by virtue of where they live (Dean and Hastings 2000). If self-respect is at least partly a product of how we are treated by others there is good reason to care about these destructive types of social relations. On this account, a further reason why policy-makers should care about the impact of local social relations on our personal development is not only because those experiences mould how we see ourselves and others, but because such perceptions in turn shape and limit the opportunities available to us.

The third and simplest reason why local social relations should matter to policy-makers is because they matter to us, the residents. A sense of local identity and pride in where you live is something we value, even if we only notice this where it is lacking (Forrest and Kearns, 1999). Trusting or at least not fearing other residents is an important part of local quality of life. Even more positively, some residents might actively appreciate feeling that there is a local 'sense of community', or can enjoy the 'vibrancy' or 'buzz' of an area that is characterised by a diverse social mix. Social relationships generally are not entered into because we objectively calculate what we can get out of them, but simply because we enjoy each other's company or just happen to cross paths every so often. None of this means that we have to be close friends with our neighbours or even that we should know them enough to like or dislike them. It just means that people appreciate sharing minimally civil and decent social relations with their neighbours or feeling some sense of belonging. Life is just easier and more pleasant if we have these things.

As well as mattering to individuals, commitment to place can also benefit the general public and government. Such commitment is more likely to stimulate the sense of responsibility that encourages people to look after their living environment, resulting in streets and spaces that are pleasant for everyone to use. When people feel happy in the place where they live, they can feel that they have an investment in the area, and consequently will be less likely to want to leave should conditions deteriorate or may even be willing to make some contribution to prevent that deterioration. The converse is also true. In areas which are already physically run down or neglected residents are more likely to lack commitment to the place, feeling that further deterioration is unpreventable or unimportant. Tony Blair referred to this as the 'broken window' problem arguing that a failure to tackle small-scale problems such as graffiti and vandalism can signal the absence of local commitment or responsibility and eventually lead to anti-social behaviour or more serious criminality (Blair 2001). Physical decay can speed social decay, but the social strength of 'community' or local commitment to place can inhibit processes of physical deterioration. In this light, local and central government may benefit materially from local commitment to place because any strengthening of local social responsibility could lower the costs of street-cleaning, maintenance work or even policing.

The discussion in this section is intended to show why community matters and why it should be a concern of public policy. The suggestion was that 'community' refers to the relationships between people, whether within an area or in a group. These relationships contribute significantly to individual welfare and quality of life. The relationships we experience in the area where we live are of particular importance not because they are necessarily very emotionally significant, but simply because they provide lots of things we value. In this sense the focus on community goes one step further than Putnam's arguments for social capital in that it recognises the extra value of social resources being generated within a particular area.

Before moving on to pin down exactly what sort of local social relations public policy should be concerned with it is worth summarising the findings of this section. The suggestion is that there are three key ways in which positive local social relations can produce policy-relevant benefits for individuals and the state. Those three types of benefit are:

- Social capital or network effects – who you know and how well you know them matters. Things that we value such as social support, mutual aid, financial help, or information about jobs are provided by local social relationships. On a broader scale, social capital across an area may be associated with better health or crime outcomes, or even improved economic performance; high levels of local trust are particularly valuable.

- Socialisation effects – the social environment in which we live or grow up can exert unconscious pressure on our values, expectations and perceptions. If people are to grow up with mainstream values and aspirations, or without a sense of stigmatisation or discriminatory outlook, then they need to experience positive role model effects especially during childhood.

- Attachment effects – living somewhere which gives us a sense of belonging, identity or commitment can have the important psychological effect of simply making us feel good. But the effects of such attachment to place can translate into more tangible benefits such as higher levels of social responsibility and trust, which can help maintain the local public environment, keep crime levels low and even make local co-operation easier.

Community as a policy goal

The suggestion is not only that should we care about the character of social relations, but we should also be concerned with the possible benefits of a certain desirable type of social relations, namely those that could be described as community of place. In many ways this is the most difficult step to take. It is relatively easy to lay out the reasons why we should take account of the effects of public policy on local social relations, but it is much more controversial to suggest that policy-makers should care about a particular sort of relations that we will call 'community'. Although as noted at the start of this chapter 'community' tends to evoke positive ideas of friendship, trust and solidarity, it is a concept that can also have a more sinister edge. Much academic debate has focused on this dark side of community and these concerns are practical as well as theoretical, referring to the negative aspects of real-life close-knit communities. In order to defend the claim that community should be an important policy goal we need to show that this 'darker side' can be avoided.

A good starting point is to decide whether there are any limits as to what sorts of social relations qualify as a community. Although the academic study of politics has argued for centuries over what 'community' means, there tends to be a common thread that can be observed in thinkers as different as Aristotle, Locke and Giddens. The common thread is that of *something shared*. Different thinkers give different accounts of what has to be shared in order for relationships to count as community. The most important difference is between accounts which present a fairly value-free descriptive view, and those which more ambitiously attach a value-laden meaning. Mason, for example, offers two versions – an ordinary concept and a moralised concept. In the first of these, community 'is constituted by a group of people who share a range of values, a way of life, identify with the group and its practices and recognise each other as members of that group.' (Mason 2000: 21) The moralised concept is even more demanding: 'First, there must be solidarity between its members... Second, there must be no systematic exploitation or...no systematic injustice.' (Mason 2000: 27)

What type of social relations should we value as 'community' relations at the neighbourhood level? The answer to this question must bear in mind that British political tradition, like that of other liberal states, tends to assume that the state shouldn't interfere too excessively in individuals' lives and choices. So whilst it might be appealing to think that of course local relations should be close, solidaristic and non-exploitative, we also have to recognise that the reach of the state into people's lives would have to be extended a great deal in order to bring about such a situation.

I would suggest that at minimum, we can't avoid using something like a less demanding version of Mason's first definition but that for good policy reasons, we need to make some value judgement as to what sort of relations can count. Many definitions of community place great importance on solidarity and similarity, harking back to the sociological distinction drawn by Tonnies in the aftermath of the industrial revolution, which distinguished between strong traditional blood or land-based community, and the looser contract-based social order of new towns (Tönnies 1957). Nostalgic visions of community now often evoke traditional working-class neighbourhoods of the early 20th century. Certainly these areas may have been characterised by strong, close supportive relationships between neighbours and families but they could also be very intolerant of faces that didn't 'fit in' and were often highly inward-looking. This vision of community as made up of lots of strong bonds between like people is an inappropriate model for a 21st century vision of community. It is inappropriate both politically because of its tendency towards intolerance, and (for reasons that Marilyn Taylor's paper will reveal), also practically because it doesn't necessarily provide the sort of social resources that we may need.

At minimum then, government cannot introduce community-friendly policies that encourage individuals to be discriminatory, intolerant or racist. This suggests that the sort of community relations public policy can promote must be *civil, tolerant and decent*. Given the extensive range of benefits associated with high levels of local trust, we might also wish to add that those relations should also display trust.

This solves the matter of how value-laden a policy understanding of community should be, but it doesn't say anything at all about what it is that local residents must share in the first place. Do local residents share a range of values or a way of life? Is there any sense in which neighbours will identify with each other? Again these ideas may sound very appealing, but is worth being aware of what we can and can't reasonably expect of people. It is desirable for local residents to share a range of values, if this means having a common concern for standards of decent behaviour, basic mutual respect and some overlapping vision of how the neighbourhood should be maintained as Elizabeth Frazer elucidates further in Chapter 3. It would, however, be highly undesirable to suppose that residents should share the same sets of personal values, whether those be grounded in religious beliefs, political ideologies or sexual identity.

There is one other thing that local residents could usefully share. The previous section pointed out the benefits of a sense of belonging or commitment to place. It was suggested that this feeling might contribute in an important if intangible way to an individual's quality of life. In so far as such a sense of investment would also make individuals more likely to look after there area or take an interest in the quality of local services there would appear to be clear policy benefits in promoting this sort of feeling.

Putting these two claims together we could suggest that a definition of community of place appropriate to policy needs would be:

> Social relations of a trusting and civil nature, where those relationships are grounded in a shared commitment to the neighbourhood or area.

In other words, if policy-makers are concerned to promote community of place they should ensure that policies promote trusting and civil social relations at the local level, and where applicable, that they help to cultivate a common sense of place and belonging. Although not strictly part of the definition, issues raised earlier in this paper suggest that whereas community has often been seen as characterising close, bonding ties to like others, a more contemporary interpretation of 'community of place' should recognise the value of *multiple overlapping weak and strong ties.*

What community-sensitive policy might look like

Having both defended the reasons why we should be concerned with community of place and presented a rigorous and appropriate definition it just remains to offer some insight into how public policy might support and foster community. The other contributions in this book all offer their own interpretation. Perri 6's paper suggests that thinking about social networks is the most defensible approach. Elizabeth Frazer's chapter argues that certain local policy outcomes will only be achieved if we recognise the type of social relations that are required to support them. Both Robina Goodlad and Marilyn Taylor look critically at regeneration policy and ask respectively, where it has been successful and where it has failed in maintaining a community-sensitive approach.

More generally though, it would be helpful to lay out some basic principles for a community-sensitive approach to policy-making. The following list (although not comprehensive) gives some examples of the types of principle which could underlie public policy or service delivery if they were designed to preserve or foster positive local social relations. Ultimately a more sophisticated approach would involve the development of both a rigorous community-proofing tool against which new measures could be tested for their 'community-friendliness', as well as perhaps a set of 'Best Value' style community indicators that would allow central and local government to monitor the effect of current services and initiatives.

Minimal erosion of valuable social networks

Almost every policy will exert some sort of effect on social networks. This may result from provision of a good that restricts certain sorts of connection, just as traditional British social housing policy concentrated the lowest-income individuals and families on the same estates, separating them from members of other income groups. It may result from provision of choice – it has been argued that the current policy of parental choice of school reduces the likelihood that local families will meet and form ties at the neighbourhood school gate (Worpole 2000). The provision of incentives can affect who we interact with as might be achieved where local sports or arts facilities are subsidised. Probation services or Institutions for Young Offenders are examples where certain ties are formed with others as a result of enforcement. It would thus be almost impossible to design a policy that would have an entirely neutral effect on social networks. In the context of minimising harm to 'community' and attaining some of the benefits outlined above there might be two key criteria which could be used to assess policy proposals:

- Does the policy rupture/ inhibit the development of either weak or strong social ties which are valued for their provision of, say, mutual support, informal care or information?

- Does the policy support the formation of the sort of social ties that will be most useful in achieving the policy aim?

Perri 6's paper addresses this issue in far more depth in the next chapter.

Support for positive socialisation effects

Once again, almost every policy will, at least indirectly have some effect on our individual experiences and outlook. In order to ensure that policy is sensitive to the effects it will have on socialisation and character development we would want to know the short to medium-term effects of a policy on the inhabitants of a certain area. How does it affect the range of role models available? What is portrayed as a 'normal' way of life? How does it encourage individuals to see themselves and other groups? These sort of questions are particularly important in the context of the summer disturbances in Burnham, Bradford and Oldham. If the aim is to build a cohesive and integrated society, then more attention must be paid to how children can develop tolerant and non-stereotyped views of others.

No erection of barriers to positive interaction between different groups

The barriers in question here fall in to two categories – social and physical. In order for new social ties to form or for positive socialisation experiences to develop, interaction experiences should be possible and positive. Positive social interaction can be hindered by policy initiatives which either erect effective barriers that inhibit interaction, or which exacerbate tension or distrust between existing groups. Social barriers to positive interaction might include the maintenance of language barriers, etiquette or customs of behaviour which make it hard for one group to join in. Other barriers might include some public consultation measures which pit divided groups against each other. Physical barriers to positive interaction cover factors as simple as transport or housing patterns which can effectively isolate different groups by making certain areas hard to reach. A simple principle to maintain might be that social relations within an area should not be distorted by physical disconnection of areas within it, nor by dislocation from surrounding areas. Services should also be easily accessible by all social groups, safeguarding opportunities for participation in social, civic and political life.

Preservation of spaces and places for public interaction

This covers not just outdoor spaces such as public squares or parks, but also any indoor spaces which are areas of genuine public use. Thus public libraries would count, also shopping malls, Post Offices or health centres. Contact and interaction are necessary in order for people to build social ties or to experience the effects of mixing with different others. Such contact can be minimal and still be valuable – shared facilities in residentially segregated areas may not build bonds between different groups but at least they encourage awareness and familiarity. As well as being much-valued local facilities, genuinely public spaces and places also have symbolic value. They can stand as examples of an area's public identity – the face it presents to the world. Policies that involve shutting down local post offices or abandoning local parks are damaging in several ways. Not only do they deprive residents of a key service and a place to cross or meet, such actions also suggest the diminishing importance of an area and its residents, and as such can undermine a local sense of pride or increase feelings of stigmatisation. Unfortunately there is already a significant move towards the privatisation of public space, from the closure of parks to the sale of sports fields for housing. This trend has luckily not yet reached the highly exclusionary levels of Los Angeles as documented so vividly by Mike Davis (Davis 1990).

Maintenance of local environmental quality

In order for the attachment effects of community to be capitalised upon, the area concerned needs to be the sort of place that people can feel a sense of pride in or commitment towards. A sense of local pride or identity need not stem from an attractive physical environment or sites of special interest but these certainly help.

Certainly if the physical environment is unkempt and dirty, there will be little reason for residents to feel any sense of responsibility towards it themselves. Further to this, living in such areas can have a negative psychological impact on people's self-respect. Time and again, surveys by local authorities show that what people really care about in terms of service provision are street cleaning and rubbish collection. The recent introduction of a liveability agenda goes some way towards addressing these issues, but it is important to apply the same thinking to issues of planning and design as well as routine maintenance.

Conclusion

This chapter has sought to lay the foundations for a more community-aware approach to public policy. The argument has been made that community of place matters to individuals and that it should matter to government. Not only will somewhere feel like a pleasant place to live if residents are civil and trusting towards each other, it will also probably be a safer, healthier and more prosperous place too. Long term public policy goals such as increased educational achievement or more effective local government will also be supported if the literature on social capital is to be believed. Local services such as education or street-cleaning may also benefit from the input of a populace who are committed to their area and who are prepared to take some of the responsibility for improving the quality of services delivered.

All these claims may seem far too good to be true. Certainly a degree of caution is required. Community is not some marvellous cure-all that can immediately alleviate severe policy problems, and improved health, education or crime outcomes won't be achieved through supportive social relations alone. The argument rather is that long-term policy goals such as these cannot be secured without focus on the quality of local social relations. Just as regeneration policy now acknowledges that physical, economic and social investment is required to turn around a deprived area, so we must recognise that public services cannot be improved simply by pouring more money in. The quality of local services can be raised by ensuring that residents are prepared to invest time and effort in communicating their needs to service deliverers or by using existing facilities responsibly so that money is not wasted on unnecessary use. Such a sense of social responsibility will only come where residents feel some commitment to their area, or where they trust others enough to co-operate for mutual gain. At the most basic level, an area where civil communication has broken down is unlikely to be a place where residents feel any compulsion to maintain the quality of public spaces or services used in common.

Community then must matter to policy-makers on several levels. At the broadest level a concern for community must be mainstreamed so that the effect of initiatives on local social relations is considered in all major policy decisions. Without this mainstreaming, specific initiatives to improve local social relations will be fighting a losing battle. At the next level, certain policy goals such as crime reduction require particularly careful attention to the ways in which local community of place can be supported. If the practice of policing, for example, is not designed, monitored and evaluated in a way that supports community of place then valuable resources spent on dealing with existing crime are probably wasted. At the most specific level we may need on occasion to introduce measures to rebuild community where it has already broken down. In this context it will be vital to understand what sort of 'social' aims are appropriate. One criticism that could be made of existing social regeneration policy in Britain is that it focuses too heavily on capacity-building and too little on simply building trust and communication between residents. In order for there to be local groups whose 'capacity' or skills and confidence can be built, there have to be individuals who are willing to communicate and interact together in the first place.

Endnotes

1   Although some policies can have a dramatic effect on such communities of interest as Bush's recent policy on the involvement of faith-based groups in welfare service delivery shows.

2   This has particular relevance in a multi-cultural society where different ethnic groups may use subtly different body language which others can mistakenly see as threatening or untrustworthy.

3   It is difficult to establish a clear difference between social capital and social network approaches. They are not mutually exclusive, in fact it might be most appropriate to say that social networks are a subset of the resources that social capital refers to. Thus social capital can describe both the norms, trust and networks available in an area, and the particular social network or grid of social relationships which an individual enjoys.

References

Blair T (2001) *Improving Your Local Environment* speech delivered at Groundwork Conference, Croydon

Coleman J (1988) *The Foundations of Social Theory* Massachusetts: Harvard University Press

Davis M (1992) *Cities of Quartz* London: Vintage

Dean J and Hastings A (2000) *Challenging Images: Housing Estates, Stigma and Regeneration* Bristol: The Policy Press

Forrest R & Kearns A (1999) *Joined-Up Places? Social Cohesion and Neighbourhood Regeneration* York: Joseph Rowntree Foundation

Fukuyama F (1995) *Social Capital and the Global Economy* Foreign Affairs 74(5)

Glen (1993) 'Methods and themes in community practice', in Butcher H, Glen A, Henderson P and Smith J (eds) *Community and Public Policy* London: Pluto Press

Halpern D (1999) *Social Capital: The New Golden Goose* Cambridge (unpublished review)

Hogg MA and Abrams D (1988) *Social Identifications* London: Routledge

Home Office (2001a) *Building Cohesive Communities: A report of the Ministerial Group on Public Order and Community Cohesion* London

Home Office (2001b) *A Report of the Independent Review Team* chaired by Ted Cantle London

Kawachi I, Kennedy BP and Lochner K (1997) *Long Live Community: Social Capital and Public Health* American Prospect 35 (Nov-Dec)

Mason A (2000) *Community, Solidarity and Belonging* Cambridge: CUP

Miller N and Brewer MB (1984) *Groups in Contact: The Psychology of De-segregation* Orlando: Academic Press

Putnam R (1995) *Making Democracy Work* Princeton: Princeton University Press

Putnam R (2001) *Bowling Alone* New York: Simon & Schuster

Social Exclusion Unit (SEU) (2000a) *National Strategy for Neighbourhood Renewal: A Framework for Consultation* London: Cabinet Office

Social Exclusion Unit (SEU) (2000b) *Report of Policy Action Team 8: Anti-Social Behaviour* London: Cabinet Office

Social Exclusion Unit (SEU) (2001) *A New Commitment to Neighbourhood Renewal* London: Cabinet Office

Tönnies F (1957) *Community and Society* Translated Loomis, CP Michigan: Michigan State University

Wilmott P (1989) *Community Initiatives* London: Policy Studies Institute

Worpole K (2000) *Linking Home and School* London: Demos

II: The added value of a community focus

2. Governing friends and acquaintances: public policy and social networks
Perri 6

In the last ten years or so, the argument has been made very widely that government ought to try to influence the patterns of their citizens' friendships and acquaintance, to stimulate them not only to develop more friendships and wider acquaintance but also to create incentives to have the 'right' kinds of friendships and acquaintance with other people. 'Building social capital' or 'cultivating civil society' are the principal slogans under which these arguments are made, although the degree of policy activism called for varies sharply (compare Putnam 2000, Chapter 24 with Fukuyama 1999, 274ff). Describing these ideas as government influencing friendship and acquaintance might seem tendentious – a deliberately hostile representation, perhaps. In this article, I shall not in fact offer a wholesale rejection of these ideas. However, I shall argue that these arguments cannot be justified at all unless they can be shown to be acceptable when put into these terms. Either there are good reasons for thinking that in some specified and presumably limited ways, our friendships and our acquaintances are the business of government, or else the idea that 'social capital' or 'civil society' are appropriate targets for public policy must be rejected.

These are not entirely new ideas. More common than the argument that cultivating certain patterns of friendship among citizens should be a goal of well-designed policy has been the claim that those patterns of friendship are the pre-condition of an accountable polity, as both Aristotle and Rousseau argued. The claim that government should try to shape the social networks that bind their citizens to each other is a recent twist added by communitarians (Etzioni, 1993) to the classical republican idea that civic virtue had to be fostered and sanctioned by public institutions, but a twist that would surely have given the seventeenth century republicans some anxiety.

For friendship and acquaintance are personal matters, generally exclusive and partial, even arbitrary. Most views of politics and public policy, including both classical liberalism and republicanism of both left and right stress the importance of choices being made, desert being established, and goals being pursued on the basis of impersonal, impartial and open systems, in which exactly who one is and who one happens to know are all irrelevant. Moreover, most views of politics propose some limits to the acceptable intrusiveness of public policy into areas of life, variously defined that they deem private, or areas where individual choice is deemed authoritative, whatever the consequences of choices made there for other people.

While the friendship of conspirators and the acquaintance of thieves with their 'fences' is something upon which society frowns, in general, the sanctions of law and policy have been directed to the punishment of criminal acts rather than criminal bonds. In the same way, while the benefits of friendship for good health and education are well understood, most people would shudder at the thought of a National Friendship Service.

This article sets out an argument about just how far we should want government to go in pursuing such goals. In doing so, I shall largely eschew the language of 'social capital'. For the term is dangerously inexact. Considered as a concept of social structure, it lumps together friendship and acquaintance, and indeed several quite distinct forms of each of those, when in fact making distinctions between forms is vital both for intelligent public policy and indeed for adequate understanding. Considered more generally, it is used to lump together matters of social structure at the micro-level – social networks – with principles of a moral kind – such as norms of trust or reciprocity or mutuality – with larger scale structures such as community (eg Putnam 1993 and 2000). These things do not necessarily or even typically run together. The result of using a single term for them is to reduce analysis to rhetoric. In this article, I confine my argument to a particular aspect of social structure – namely, social networks of friendship and acquaintance between individuals. By an individual's 'social network', I mean the set of ties of friendship and acquaintance to other people that are available to that individual.

I shall consider first the range of policy fields in which certain patterns of friendship and acquaintance might be so beneficial that, if government can legitimately influence them, it should do so. However, I shall argue that *all good things do not go together*: forms of social networks which may be beneficial for some goals that policy makers care about, may not be good for other goals and may even undermine them. Where there are conflicts of this kind, if government may try to influence these patterns of ties at all, then choices or trade-offs must be made. The basis on which government efforts to shape friendship and acquaintance can be justified (subject to appropriate and rather strict constraints), is that it is unavoidable that government will always influence the shape and nature of social networks, and that there is no greater virtue is doing so 'unintentionally' than in doing so with some care. Next, the article sets out a brief argument about what kinds of goals might be acceptable and what kinds of restrictions ought to be in place to limit the intrusiveness of public policy in this area. A taxonomy of the principal tools available to policy makers with which to influence social networks is then offered. Finally, a number of specific policy recommendations are offered in the fields of employment, education and some other areas of social policy, that would meet the standards set out.

Networks as policy challenges

If government may or should use the tools of public policy to shape social networks, then the first stage in the argument must involve identification of the types of social network configuration that are known to help support key public policy goals. There is now a body of evidence that has been collected over many decades which suggests that social network configurations matter in explaining the outcomes that policy makers care most about. I shall call this body of work, 'outcome research' for short.

There is good evidence that social network configurations are significant causal factors in explaining at least the following important outcomes that policy makers care about:

- patterns of epidemiology in health (eg Brunner 1996; Wilkinson 1996);

- ability and/or willingness to engage in positive health-related behaviours and/or abstain from negative ones (Morrow 1999; Franssen and Knipscheer 1990);

- the sense of security or fear among older people about their neighbourhood (Phillipson et al 1999);

- delinquency and criminality or their avoidance (eg Emler and Reicher 1995; Baron and Tindall 1993);

- educational attainment or drop-out (Teachman et al 1996, 1997);

- homelessness (eg Boulton 1993);

- general well-being and quality of life (eg Kef et al 2000; Acock and Hurlbert 1993);

- labour market attainment (eg Granovetter 1973, 1995 [1974], 1982; Gallie et al 1994);

- inter-class upward and downward mobility, including blocked mobility (eg Breiger 1990, 1995; Goldthorpe et al 1987; 6 2001);

- vulnerability to poverty (eg 6 1997a; Gordon et al 2000);

- vulnerability to frailty and difficulties in coping in extreme old age (Wenger 1997, 2000; Wenger et al 2000)

- community development (eg Crow and Allan 1994; Taylor 1996); and

- community ability to achieve collective action around local environmental concerns (Pennington and Rydin 1999).

The general finding of this research can summed up briefly in the slogan 'it's not just who you know: it's how you know them' (6 1997a). Social networks of certain forms (defined and measured by differences in size, number of ties of certain 'strengths', density of interconnection, geographical extent, diversity of membership by class and occupation) provide key resources. Ties of friendship and acquaintance can provide information about, or actual offers of jobs or business opportunities (both legitimate and criminal), or about new products, or they can directly pass infectious bacteria and viruses. They can be important persuaders for certain kinds of attitudes and preferences, set examples that may be followed at least in part, provide practical support when in need ranging from care to cash, or they can lead to other contacts not previously known who may be able to provide these things.

To the extent, then, that we expect social policy to promote health and combat disease, to promote both employment and employability, to postpone the onset of morbidity and enhance people's ability to cope with it when it arrives, to assist people from lower social classes to rise, to promote and assist the formation of new firms, then policy design must also be sensitive to those characteristics of social networks that are causally related to these outcomes and risks.

Network conflicts

For many important outcomes, however, it is not at all straightforward to disentangle the positive features of social network configurations from the negative ones. For example, the social network forms that sustain good health may also be the very ones through which communicable diseases pass; likewise, the friendship networks that may be important in maturation and school age children's academic attainment may also be the very ones that could influence the risk of delinquency or drug use. Adults who seek to change their health habits or to 'go straight' after involvement in crime may deliberately choose to lose their previous social ties, and suffer other negative consequences of isolation. This suggests that there are important trade-offs and potentially even tragic conflicts between different configurations of social network in relation to different outcomes that we might value.

That is to say, all good things do not necessarily go together in the relationship between network forms and the full set of desirable outcomes. Some configurations of personal social networks may help us to cope with some risks but may prove unhelpful or positively disabling for dealing with others. Two key areas of possible conflict can be identified.

First, it is now reasonably well established that, with some qualifications, labour market attainment is powerfully affected by the individual's ability to make use of a rich set of ties to acquaintances – rather than close friends – whose labour market situations differ from their own (Granovetter 1973, 1995 [1974]; Burt 1992). However, both for an individual over the life course and for a geographical community, having mainly weak ties does not help in the pursuit of other kinds of goals, and indeed, may actively undermine the achievement of those goals. For example, there is evidence that, at the very least, a mix of strong and weak ties is important for well-being in old age (Wenger 1997a & b, 2000) and that strong ties to peers are important in successful maturation in adolescence (Cotterell 1996). Since the main benefits from weak ties are found to be in adult life when people are generally seeing work and greater current income, this might not matter if people generally make smooth transitions in late adolescence or on retirement from one pattern of friendship and acquaintance to another (6 1997a).

However, many people do not. The networks forms which aid exit from unemployment and labour market attainment differ greatly from those which can help to postpone the onset of frailty in later life or help one to cope well with it when it does set in. Those with independent life styles, mainly weak ties and living far from children and other relatives can sometimes find it harder to manage the transition into old age for these very reasons. The deliberate cultivation, during the 'third age' of active retirement, of new ties to neighbours and other friends living nearby can be a promising option, at least for some and particularly for childless people (Wenger et al 2000).

In any case, there are other tensions between goals that call for incompatible network forms. Typically, individuals with networks mainly composed of weak ties to people in situations different from their own will not have many ties to people in their own neighbourhood. The casual nature of acquaintance does not lend itself to the more intense trust required for prolonged collective action and the kinds of high commitment and organisation building that are often required in local community development. This makes for a potential tension between the network requirements of individual labour market attainment and collective local community activism. The 'weak tie' factors that make for individual labour market success might be at least ambivalent for community development. Certainly, leaders in community-based organisations need a range of weak links with people in relevant political authorities, commercial organisations and large formal voluntary bodies, in order to access resources to bring back to their communities. But the effectiveness, and indeed the goals of community development turn as much as – or more – on the strength, duration and density of the ties within the community as on the links through which a small number of leaders broker external resources. A local community that relies for its development solely on leaders with good external links will soon find those leaders offered jobs elsewhere or promoted into statutory sector roles, so reducing an area's capacity for self-regeneration.

Impacts of policy on networks

Employment, employability, educational success, avoidance of crime or frailty, well organised communities and the like are all desirable goals, but even if government intervention is seen as legitimate, can it actually influence the social network forces that so powerfully affect the achievement of these goals? The argument that it can do so proceeds in three distinct stages. The first stage is to show that government cannot avoid affecting the patterns of friendship and acquaintance between citizens. The second is to show that there is no greater virtue in doing so unintentionally than in doing so with care. The third is to show that government possesses a range of quite specific tools with which to influence social networks. Having established this, it will be possible to consider how far it may do so, what constraints it should be subject to, and what goals might be acceptable.

Governments have enormous influence over the patterns of social ties in their populations. This influence is most obvious in those areas of domestic policy activity that are conventionally defined as falling within the 'welfare state', but is by no means confined to social policy. Certainly, housing policy programmes have created and destroyed geographical communities, shaping and even dramatically shaking up the social networks of local authority and housing association tenants (as during slum clearance and re-housing, or during temporary 'decanting' for repairs). Land use planning has similarly reshaped the social networks of owner occupiers. The practice of accommodating many homeless families in hostels and in bed and breakfast hotels on a temporary basis creates denser networks among these families than with other groups, with potentially large consequences. Similar effects are seen in the field of employment policy where practices of providing segregated vocational training programmes for unemployed people has enabled people to form links only with people in similarly depressed situations whose access to useful information about work or housing is often no better than their own.

'Care in the community' for people with serious mental illnesses has, in practice, often meant living in supervised group homes which has created very particular patterns of social ties for these groups, often rather separated from wider society. On the other side in disputes about the siting of these facilities in residential areas, NIMBY mobilisation against homes for people needing care in the community represent one form of network change that occurs in reaction against government initiatives. Many older people face a choice between 'care in the community' and 'residential care' (which can too often mean a choice between a humane form of house arrest and acute isolation or incarceration in a group providing only the most minimal form of social contact) which will significantly affect their social network patterns. In many areas 'befriending services' are funded through voluntary organisations, in order to provide informal, low level social support networks to isolated older housebound people, people with motor and learning disabilities, people with mental illnesses, adults suffering from autism, and so on. Probation services are quite explicitly intended to have an impact on social networks, by enabling and encouraging ex-offenders and those remanded on bail to develop ties with those who have no criminal record and are unlikely to offend. In the same way, measures such as community development work on poor estates, community policing work establishing neighbourhood watch or other local counter-crime efforts and programmes of holistic or 'joined-up' government bringing together different professional groups, are all quite explicitly designed to initiate, foster and sustain social network ties between targeted individuals and groups.

Transport policies have great impacts on social networks, by making it easier or more difficult for people living in certain areas to reach and maintain contact with others through work, social visiting and so on. Perhaps the most famous case of deliberate use of transport policy to break social network ties is that of the work of the New York civil architect and planner, Robert Moses. It is said that he designed raised highways at a deliberately low height above the ground in order to prevent buses running from poor areas on local roads underneath from reaching better off parts of the city, and whose plans (it is alleged) deliberately segregated areas. The fact that Hackney, one of the poorest boroughs in London, has never had a connection with the city's underground system has also had enormous impacts on the social network ties, and hence the employment opportunities and many other outcomes, open to its residents.

Education also has enormous impacts on social network ties, as demonstrated by the plethora of means used by wealthy and middle class people to sustain contact with former school, college and university peers over their life. It is also shown graphically by the depressing literature on 'peer group pressure' and anti-intellectual cultures among groups who anticipate very low or negative returns in adult life from investment in formal qualifications. Public health policy works through social networks of ordinary citizens in order to disseminate health messages, and so deepens (or breaks) them. It also promotes new kinds of networking between health professionals, builds links between health professionals and, for example, the food production and retail industries, and other services. Curative and palliative medical programmes are often pursued through the development of self-help groups and on-line communities of sufferers from specific diseases (or their kin) with the active involvement of medical specialists.

Areas of government activity other than social policy also have enormous impacts on social networks. Trade and industry policy is heavily devoted to the creation of networks across firms within and between industries for the sharing of commercially non-sensitive good practice, the development of technical standards and joint export promotion. Arts policy is not confined to the making of grants to individuals, but is heavily involved in making links between artists within and between media. Policies toward sport ranging from financial support for particular facilities to investment in specialist training schools and colleges, through to support for sports activity within mainstream education have vast impacts on the social network structure of young people's lives.

Regulatory policies too impact upon social networks. Land use planning has already been mentioned in this context, but it should also be noted that zoning practices for night clubs, bars, restaurants and cafés and a host of other facilities designed for sociability and conviviality represent some of the most basic ways in which government influences social networks. The ways in which professions are regulated also provide good examples. State licenses for medical, legal, accounting, architecture and engineering professions are made conditional upon the development of certain kinds of internal social networking within professions which are believed, rightly or wrongly, to promote mutual learning, mutual surveillance and oversight, support, training, dissemination of innovation, peer accountability, and so on. Regulators working in the field of health and safety or data protection put at least as much effort into the development of networks of compliance officers across and within industries as they do into investigation of breaches and enforcement or imposition of sanctions.

It follows from this that even a process of wholesale withdrawal from these areas of policy, as advocated by neo-liberals to produce some minimal or 'night-watchman' state would itself have huge consequences for social networks. In any case, there is no single pristine 'natural' condition of social networks 'prior' to the civil activities of government, to which friendship and acquaintance would 'revert' on such a withdrawal. Still less is there evidence that network forms in the absence of public services would in any automatic way lead to better settlements being made between forms of networks that bring about tensions between goals.

If the argument is accepted that government cannot help affecting patterns of friendship, the question arises as to whether it make more sense for governments to try to bring some coherence to these impacts and reduce harm where possible, or whether they should simply pursue other goals and leave these effects as 'unintended' consequences. Once it is realised that behaviour is having a certain effect, it is surely disingenuous to claim that a decision to go on behaving in the same way leaves those effects 'unintended'. In general, we expect people and governments alike to reduce the harms they do once they realise what impact their behaviour has. Typically we reasonably expect them, as a result of realising what they do, to bring some greater care, thought and coherence to their actions, with these effects in mind. Certainly, it is hard to understand a claim that government does better, whether morally or simply in respect of efficacy of its policy, by recognising but then ignoring these consequences.

Of course, policy incoherence cannot always be eliminated, and there are also reasons for thinking that it should not always be. Totally logically consistent policies may not be very robust, and may not be able to recognise the full range of legitimate interests and commitments. However, there remain many areas where greater coherence in policy is not damaging and can be beneficial for the effectiveness of policy and the reduction of harms that policy might otherwise cause (6 1997b; 6 et al 2002). It is therefore necessary to ask whether government could design its policies in such a way as to bring care and coherence to the impacts that it has upon friendship and acquaintance.

Government does have tools with which to bring greater coherence to the impact of its policies upon citizens' friendship and acquaintance. It is now conventional to distinguish between four kinds of tools of government – those that effect change in behaviour (*effectors*), those that gather information (*detectors*), those that bring in resources (*collectors*), and those that analyse, sort and present information for policy-making and managing organisations (*selectors*) (Hood 1983; 6 et al 1999, 2002). Within each of these categories, tools can be ranked from strong (coercive) to weak (permissive), according to the extent of discretion they leave to those upon whom the tools are targeted. In each of these categories, there are specific tools available to government with which public policy may either deliberately or unintentionally influence the patterns of citizens' friendship and acquaintance. Figure 2.1 identifies some of the principal tools in each category. The first column identifies key general types within each of the four categories, while the second gives examples of these in relation to shaping social networks, and the third identifies some unintended effects upon networks of the use of such tools. Collectors are not relevant for this particular subject matter.

(It should be kept in mind when reading Figure 2.1, that, just because a tool is available, it does not follow that it would necessarily be right for government to use it, at least in any particular situation. Considerations of acceptability are examined in the next section.)

Neither policy evaluation studies nor social network studies have provided us with any very detailed knowledge of what can expected from the deliberate use of such tools. No doubt, as is the case more generally, there is no single absolutely general answer to the question 'what will happen if we use this particular tool?' for everything will depend on context (Linder and Peters 1998). Much more research is needed on this. However, it should be clear from this analysis, that government is not powerless to bring coherence and order to its unavoidable impacts upon citizens' friendship and acquaintance, if it can be shown that it may and should do so.

Figure 2:1: The tools of government for the shaping of social networks

	Types of tools in their general form, ranked from strong to weak	Examples of tools used more or less directly and deliberately to shape social networks	Examples of tools more or less indirectly and unintentionally shaping social networks
Effectors *(for producing changes in culture or behaviour)*	Direct government provision Government-owned corporations Regulation, mandation, permission, prohibition Rights and systems of redress Contract purchasing Loan guarantees Grants-in-aid, matching grants Tax expenditures Information delivery: persuasion, propaganda, example, demonstration projects, education, training	Compulsorily placing people in situations limiting their opportunities to meet and get to know others, or directing them to people like them (eg 'total institutions'; 'diversion' programmes for delinquents; or simply separation within schools or workplaces) Compulsory individualised friendship management eg mentoring for unemployed people, counselling as for illicit drug use (Nolan, 1998) Voluntarily offered and entered befriending schemes Encouragement and persuasion to socialise with particular persons or types of persons, not others eg in education Social skills education	Restrictions on location of residence and freedom of movement, or on ease of change of residence (eg transfer rules in social rented housing sectors) Cost of transport Labour management arrangements and nature of job contacts at work, as affected by regulation, taxation, etc (private sector) or direct management (public sector) Models of housing design, road layout, transport routing, location of collectively consumed services
Detectors *(for acquiring information)*	Requisition Inspection Purchasing, barter Appeals (including rewards for information)	Requirements to disclose names of friends and acquaintance when under criminal investigation Requirements to divulge anonymous or identified information on ties when under counselling eg unemployment counselling Voluntary disclosure eg in form to be anonymised in response to government voluntary survey	Interviews on 'peer group pressure' in education welfare, social work, probation, among young people at risk, delinquents, etc Public health promotion programmes identifying informal networks for health information distribution
Selectors *(for managing, selecting, analysing, presenting information)*	Audit Cost-benefit analysis Performance indicators and measurement Cost measurement, resource budgeting Management review Scenario-building, risk assessment	Use of sociometric mapping techniques by employment counsellors	Mapping techniques used in social services, probation, education or welfare on distribution and linkages between young people at risk, delinquents Network impact auditing on employment services, services for older people, housing programmes etc.

Acceptable goals, required constraints

If it is accepted that government cannot avoid having an impact on social networks, that there is no greater merit in doing so 'unintentionally', and that government has tools with which it might more carefully and deliberately affect the friendships and acquaintance of citizens, then we must at least briefly consider what goals might be acceptable, and what constraints should limit the scope of government's ambitions in this field.

In general people have a quite proper suspicion of governments' claims to know what is best for them better than they themselves do and this must apply to policies on the patterns of our friendships. It would surely be wrong for public policy to seek to promote any single vision of the 'correct' pattern of friendship and acquaintance for citizens, or indeed any group of citizens, whether socially excluded or otherwise. The goal of policy surely ought to be to allow as wide a range of choice and pluralism as is compatible with a viable polity (Rawls, 1993). It is this which, I believe, probably makes the present argument incompatible with communitarianism, for communitarians do believe that there is a single correct configuration social network, which they call 'community', which they demand that government use its powers to promote.

It follows from this bias against promoting a single preferred pattern of social ties, that any imposition of enforceable duties upon individuals to form or use certain kinds of networks – for example, on pain of loss of state benefits – would require special justification (see below). This suggests that goals should principally be negative in character. That is to say, government should focus on *minimising network harm* – reducing the conditions in which citizens face social network forms that do not allow them to pursue their interests. (This is subject to the proviso that there will be some conflicts and trade-offs where combating one type of 'network harm' will conflict with combating another.) But even negative goals may not be pursued by any means. At the very least, in a field such as friendship and acquaintance that is widely and properly regarded as within the citizens' sphere of 'personal' choices there ought to be at the least the following constraints upon public policy:

- Weak tools should be preferred to strong, wherever possible, in order to respect liberty as far as possible.

- The detectors chosen should be the fewest necessary, in order to respect privacy as far as possible.

- Specific policy justification in terms of specific harms should be given or at least available for the use of each tool, and should be subject to the general and very limited conditions under which paternalism can be justified (6 2000a).

- Policies that would impose duties on individuals to seek or to use social ties for particular purposes – for example, in job search and subject to the sanction of withdrawal of benefit – should be subject to requirements for special additional justification (6 2000b).

- Tools should be no stronger and policies no more extensive than is appropriate for the scale of the harm to be combated.

- Citizens should have clear and specific rights of redress for abuse of power in the course of the deployment of tools to shape their social networks.

- Disadvantaged citizens should not be disproportionately targeted in such policies.

- Such policies should be transparently undertaken, limited to the goals set and not designed in ways that are manipulative, whether by pursuing ulterior goals or by deceiving citizens.

- The legislature should provide itself with institutional means to exercise frequent vigilance over the intrusiveness of such policies.

It is sometimes argued that there is an irreconcilable conflict between, on the one hand, support for the use of informal social ties as a route into the labour market from unemployment or in promotion and upward mobility, and, on the other, a commitment to equal opportunities. On one particular interpretation of the goals of equal opportunities, perhaps this might be true. However, if equal opportunities policy is understood more broadly as biting on distributive justice in *outcomes*, rather than principally on reliance upon particular *processes* using exclusively formal labour institutions, then it should be possible to ask organisations to demonstrate their compliance with equal opportunities principles in their use of personal networks, just as we do now about their use of formal recruitment institutions. It is a misconception that justice cannot be reconciled with policies that recognise particularism (O'Neill 1996).

Policy directions

Within these constraints and with this goal of reducing harms, there are nevertheless important and urgent tasks for public policy. For there are many respects in which current policy programmes could be causing significant problems that affect opportunities for upward social mobility, particularly for unemployed people. In this section, I shall therefore briefly present some policy options that could be adopted by British government to minimise network harm. I first examine the harmful effects of existing programmes directed at the unemployed and socially excluded, where existing programmes undermine their ability to use social networks to get into work and to improve their labour market attainment. Secondly, I shall go on to present ideas that tackle some of the barriers to working class children forming ties with middle class children, which may affect their sense of self-efficacy and are also important for aspiration, upward mobility and labour market attainment (see also 6 1997a, 2001).

The studies on job search and on upward social mobility from the poorest income deciles find consistently that weak ties are crucial – that is, ties to people unlike oneself, in different situations, and with access to information about work that one could not readily find for oneself. Yet too many current programmes do little for or even undermine the ability of unemployed people to develop and sustain such ties. For example, in the course of most welfare-to-work programmes, rather little support is given to unemployed people in assisting them to use informal routes into work which are often the most effective. Indeed, the incentives for local Employment Service offices are typically to route clients into work using only the Service's own formal routes. Most job readiness and training programmes put unemployed people only in touch with other unemployed people. Even some subsidised work options have been found to segregate New Deal placement workers from other staff, limiting their opportunities for forming ties. A number of specific options for policy changes to the New Deal therefore suggest themselves:

- Personal advisors should ensure that at the point of diagnosis, mentors take responsibility for assisting clients with thinking through how they might use their existing social ties to find work; however, details of named individuals should not be recorded.

- Personal advisors and mentors should discuss with clients the opportunities that work and training options might afford for making new social ties that might be of value in future job search and network resources to support longer term employability and not just short term employment.

- The experience of the New Deal should be evaluated in significant part for its impact on the network contribution to employability, by asking clients at the end of the Gateway or subsidised work, how many more people they now know to whom they might turn for information about work opportunities, as a result of the programme.

However, there are many other areas of policy activity that can negatively affect the social network situation of people who are at risk of unemployment, poverty and social exclusion. Therefore, an audit of policy would also have to include some of the longer term, more preventive options. The following are some areas it would be important to explore:

- Support to young people in local authority care should concentrate on overcoming harms to social networks through isolation and through lack of either strong or weak ties.

- Transport planning priorities should reflect the importance of overcoming problems of disconnection for estates of low income housing.

- Land use planning, housing investment and community development programmes should focus on supporting residential communities with a variety of leisure and other facilities for social mixing and for sustaining contact with outsiders, and especially with people who are better off. Although hopes may have been overblown for supporting social networks through mixed tenure design, both because residential settings are not the most important ones for social contact in British society and because tenure divisions can reflect deeper social divisions, it remains important to limit the damage to the social fabric that can be brought about by poorly thought out spatial policy.

- Rehabilitation programmes for ex-offenders should specifically address the development of social ties between ex-offenders and the wider community, and not only design services that put ex-offenders in touch with each other. Recent trends in the design of probation work to integrate its goals more closely with retribution and control have, unfortunately, undermined capacity to achieve this.

Some people argue for extension of community service programmes for young people, and even for compulsory community service. The argument is that these schemes put working class and middle class young people cheek by jowl, and out of such shared work and living, they hope, will come ties that will be of real instrumental value to working class people later in life. At best, the evidence for this claim is limited. As an extrapolation from the evidence about volunteering and mobility (Goldthorpe *et al* 1987), it is vulnerable to the doubt that large-scale and compulsory schemes may have quite different effects upon social ties than small-scale and voluntary ones do. Moreover, the evidence from National Service and conscription suggests that class divisions tend to be perpetuated within such large-scale programmes, and that, even where they are not, social mixing and the building of lasting ties, that are or can be successfully invoked in later life, cannot be relied upon. The most that could be said for the possible effects of such schemes upon employment and mobility might be an argument that participation could enhance self-confidence for some working class and poor participants, which might show up in higher aspirations and willingness to bear risks to support those aspirations. There may, of course, be other arguments for such schemes, that are not concerned with network effects upon employment and mobility.

Although social ties formed at school may not last into adult life, and so may not be of direct instrumental importance as weak ties for the passing of information about job opportunities, ties across class lines at schools may well be indirectly important. There is some evidence that the sense of self-confidence and self-efficacy that middle-class children are supported in, may 'rub off' to some degree on working class children in socially mixed schools. Unfortunately, of course, the strategies employed by middle class parents in respect of their children's schooling often have the effect, either deliberately or unintentionally, of enforcing class separation. Although there are important regional differences, many middle class parents are able to protect their less bright children from what might otherwise be their educational and ultimately their labour market fate in several ways. They can buy extra tuition or private education in 'crammer' schools or move to more expensive homes in order to qualify on catchment area criteria to get those children into better schools. They can act collectively with other middle class parents to improve schools through fundraising and can ensure that their children attend schools where they will principally meet other middle class children thus reinforcing their confidence and developing their middle class social networks. Another possibility later on down the line is for middle class parents to use their own personal social networks to find salariat work for their children and to enhance their self-confidence by reassuring their children (if only implicitly) that there would be 'cushions' in place should they take risks in order to maintain salariat lifestyles.

Clearly, the nature of the educational system permits this form of 'opportunity hoarding' (Tilly 1998) and class closure which can undermine the network resources of working class children, and can inhibit their ability to develop self-confidence through association with middle class children. However, the scope for policy action to tackle the problem is very limited. For no government in a liberal democracy can legitimately take action that curbs the ability of parents to do what they see as the best for their children, or to put the interests of other, less advantaged children before those of their own.

However, some modest measures to limit the damage that the education system allows might be explored. One option here might be to put pressure on schools to adopt wider catchment areas. This might follow the 'planning gain' principle, or the principle used by US utility regulators: schools that sought to focus on a well-off district might be required to take part of a less well-off district as well, as a kind of 'price'. Greater emphasis on value-added performance measures in the incentive system may have some positive effect in promoting upward mobility, although we are already seeing the first signs of a middle class backlash against value-added measures: some heads have recently protested that this 'penalises' them for taking bright pupils.

More controversially, if the anti-mobility effects of opportunity hoarding by the middle class cannot be combated in any other way, it may be necessary to re-open the question of whether something not wholly unlike the old Assisted Places Scheme might not have to be reintroduced. The old scheme did not, it is accepted, represent good value for money, and was neither well enough targeted nor large enough to make much impact in limiting opportunity hoarding. However, there have been intriguing proposals for better targeted schemes on a larger scale (eg Walden 1996). Although likely to be marginal in their effect upon social networks and mobility, regulatory powers might be used to require private schools to collaborate with and share certain resources with state schools.

To the extent that housing market costs in areas near good schools represent a major entry barrier and to the extent that simply investing in attracting better heads and teachers to schools in poorer areas may take too long or prove hard to sustain, there is a case for considering what more could be done to assist people from working class backgrounds to stay in the competition for owner-occupied homes in such areas. The abolition of mortgage interest tax relief, which was an evident piece of middle class welfare, is of some long term help here, but its short term effect on mobility is almost certainly marginal. The main instruments that we possess here are in the form of capital grants to those in social rented housing to move into owner occupation. However, the extent of the residualisation of these sectors after twenty years of sales means that the impact of schemes targeted on these clientèles on wider upward mobility is likely to be limited. Although its effects may only be felt in the long term, it may be that government can best open up access to some neighbourhoods via the combined use of development control policy and incentives for housing associations to purchase assets in expensive areas. Government should promote mixed tenure investment in even very small areas (expensive as this is) and accept the housing management inefficiencies of 'pepper-potting' in the social rented stock.

The argument here is not that by means such as these, government can improve, still less abolish the conflicts identified above, or that government can effectively or should promote the 'right' sorts of social networks. However, to the extent that government chooses to place its emphasis on the side of exit from unemployment, employability and upward mobility for the least advantaged, then the kinds of policies suggested here are ones that can be developed in pursuit of that goal.

Conclusion

The idea that our friendship and acquaintance is, in any part, the business of government, is one that rightly causes unease. There are two sources of that unease: one is that the state should, at least where possible, stand loftily above particularisms and the partialities of preference between persons, and the other is that it should seek to avoid intrusion into the sphere of the personal save where it must. Certainly, government should only be entrusted with responsibilities in this sphere, subject to clear, specific constraints and with institutions of vigilance against abuse.

However, public policy has little choice but to be conceived in the register of the social, as much as it is in economic and legal registers. For the programmes that civil government commissions will unavoidably shape the patterns of friendship and acquaintance, and hence the life chances, of their citizens. Once this is accepted, there can be no argument against deploying the tools of government in this regard with greater sensitivity, deliberation, care and coherence – subject to the proviso that there are always hard choices and trade-offs to be made, and that there are always limitations to the extent that policy can be made completely coherent.

Some priorities for policy rethinking have been offered here, but in any such list, and whether one begins from concerns about health or crime or attainment, the contexts of education, the labour market and the geographical community must surely be among the most important arenas for more network-sensitive policy design. At the very least, it is the responsibility of government to attempt to reduce the network harms that its policies do. While we surely ought to be vigilant against the communitarians' overweening ambitions for government to take on the role of moulding us into their preferred model of community, there are quite clear ways in which, subject to clear and specific constraints, the world of friendship and acquaintance is an arena that no government can decently ignore.

References

Acock AC and Hurlbert JS (1993) 'Social networks, marital status and well-being' *Social Networks* 15, 3, 309-334

Baron SW and Tindall DB (1993) 'Network structure and delinquent attitudes within a juvenile gang' *Social Networks* 15, 3, 255-273

Boulton I (1993) 'Youth homelessness and health care', in Fisher K and Collins J (eds) 1993 *Homelessness, Health Care and Welfare Provision* Routledge, London, 136-148

Breiger R (ed) (1990) *Social Mobility and Social Structure* Cambridge University Press, Cambridge

Breiger R(1995) 'Social structure and the phenomenology of attainment' *Annual Review of Sociology* 21, 115-136

Brunner E (1996) 'The social and biological basis of cardiovascular disease in office workers' in Blane D, Brunner E and Wilkinson R (eds) 1996 *Health and Social Organisation: towards a health policy for the 21st century* Routledge, London, 272-299

Cotterell J (1996) *Social Networks and Social Influences in Adolescence* Routledge, London

Crow G and Allan G (1994) *Community Life: an introduction to local social relationships* Harvester Wheatsheaf (Prentice-Hall), Hemel Hempstead

Emler N and Reicher S (1995) *Adolescence and Delinquency: the collective management of reputation* Blackwell, Oxford

Etzioni A (1993) *The Spirit of Community: rights, responsibilities and the communitarian agenda* Fontana, London

Franssen M-JAMJ and Knipscheer KCPM (1990) 'Normative influences of the intimate social network on health behaviour' in Knipscheer KCPM and Antonucci TC (eds) 1990 *Social Network Research: substantive issues and methodological questions* Swets and Zeitlinger, Amsterdam

Fukuyama F (1999) *The Great Disruption: human nature and the reconstitution of social order* Profile Books, London

Gallie D, Marsh C and Vogler C (1994) *Social Change and the Experience of Unemployment* Oxford University Press, Oxford

Goldthorpe JH, Llewellyn C and Payne C (1987) *Social Mobility and Class Structure in Modern Britain* 2nd edition, Clarendon Press, Oxford University Press, Oxford

Gordon D, Townsend P, Levitas R, Pantazis C, Payne S, Patsios D, Middleton S, Ashworth K, Adelman L, Bradshaw J, Williams J and Bramley G (2000) *Poverty and Social Exclusion in Britain* Joseph Rowntree Foundation, York

Granovetter MS (1973) 'The strength of weak ties' *American Journal of Sociology* 78, 1360-1380

Granovetter MS (1995 [1974]) *Getting a Job: a study of contacts and careers* 2nd edition, University of Chicago Press, Chicago, Illinois

Granovetter MS (1982) 'The strength of weak ties: a network theory revisited' in Marsden PV, Lin N (eds) 1982 *Social Structure and Network Analysis* Sage, Beverly Hills, California, 105-130

Hood CC (1983) *The Tools of Government* MacMillan, Basingstoke

Kef S, Hox JJ and Habekothé HT (2000) 'Social networks of visually impaired and blind adolescents: structure and effect on well-being' *Social Networks* 22, 1, 73-91

Linder SH and Peters BG (1998) 'The study of policy instruments: four schools of thought' in Peters BG and van Nispen FKM (eds) 1998 *Public Policy Instruments: evaluating the tools of public administration* Edward Elgar, Cheltenham, 33-45

Morrow V (1999) 'Conceptualising social capital in relation to the health and well-being of children: a review' *Sociological Review* 47, 4, 744-765

O'Neill O (1996) *Towards Justice and Virtue: a constructive account of practical reasoning* Cambridge University Press, Cambridge

Pennington M and Rydin Y (1999) 'Researching social capital in local environmental policy contexts' *Policy and Politics* 28, 2, 233-249

Phillipson C, Bernard M, Phillips J and Oggs J (1999 'Older people's experience of community life: patterns of neighbouring in three urban areas' *Sociological Review* 47, 4, 715-743

Putnam RD with Leonardi R and Nanetti RY (1993) *Making Democracy Work: civic traditions in modern Italy* Princeton University Press, Princeton, New Jersey

Putnam RD (2000) *Bowling Alone: the collapse and revival of American community* Simon and Schuster, New York

Rawls J (1993) *Political Liberalism* Columbia University Press, New York

6 P (1997a) *Escaping Poverty: from safety nets to networks of opportunity* Demos, London

6 P (1997b) *Holistic Government* Demos, London

6 P (2000a) 'The morality of managing risk: paternalism, prevention, precaution and the limits of proceduralism' *Journal of Risk Research* 3, 2, 135-165

6 P (2000b) 'Can the obligations in welfare to work schemes be morally justified?' paper presented at the consultation on 'The morality of welfare', at St George's House, Windsor Castle, Berkshire, June 27-29, 1999

6 P (2001) 'Profiles, networks, risk and hoarding: public policy and the dynamics of social mobility and social cohesion' paper given at the Performance and Innovation Unit seminar on 'Social Mobility', Cabinet Office, London, 20 March 2001

6 P, Leat D, Seltzer K and Stoker G (1999) *Governing in the Round: strategies for holistic government* Demos, London

6 P, Leat D, Seltzer K and Stoker G (2002) *Towards Holistic Governance: the new reform agenda* Palgrave, Basingstoke

Taylor M (1996) 'Community organisations in urban regeneration: does empowerment work?' paper presented at the 25th Annual Conference of the American Research Association on Nonprofit and Voluntary Action (ARNOVA), New York, 7th-9th November, 1996

Teachman JD, Paasch K and Carver K (1996) 'Social capital and dropping out of school early' *Journal of Marriage and the Family* 58, August, 773-783

Tilly C (1998) *Durable Inequality* University of California Press, Berkeley, California

Walden G (1996) *We Should Know Better* Fourth Estate, London

Wenger GC (1997a) 'Social networks and the prediction of elderly people at risk' *Aging and Mental Health* 1, 4, 311-320

Wenger GC (2000) 'Informal support networks of older people: international perspectives' paper for HPER seminar, Indiana University, Bloomington, 2 April

Wenger GC, Scott A and Patterson N (2000) 'How important is parenthood? Childlessness and support in old age in England' *Ageing and Society* 20, 161-182

Wilkinson RG (1996) *Unhealthy Societies: the afflictions of inequality* Routledge, London

3. Local social relations: public, club and common goods

Elizabeth Frazer

A policy focus on community may be of greatest value because it encourages attention to the detail of local social relations, but it also, by the same token, reminds us of what it is that we should and do share at the local level. This paper is concerned with the various neighbourhood goods we share and the conditions in which they will thrive. The argument is that unless we take greater account of local social relations it will be difficult to ensure the provision and maintenance of communal goods such as clean, safe streets, attractive public spaces and parks. Familiar co-ordination problems such as the tragedy of the commons may help to explain why we have seen the decay of such facilities in many urban areas. Resolution of this problem may be achieved in several ways, the implications of which are explored in this paper for their impact on local social relations.

This essay begins from a number of premises. First, that quality of life where people live and work really matters. From one point of view this looks like an unexceptionable proposition, barely worth stating. However, it can be argued that the political ideal of mobility deals with the problem of local conditions by securing for individuals the freedom and the right to move from declining or unpleasant areas, to choose where to live and work. In response we can propose two distinct arguments. First that the ideal of mobility fails to address the needs of the immobile – and at several points in our life-courses each of us is immobile. Second, the negative effects of areas that are derelict or depressed affect not just the people in them, but spill out. Defensiveness, avoidance and fear are experienced well beyond the immediate physical boundaries of such areas.

Our second premise is that the relationship between individuals, and the state (national or local) and big structures like 'the economy' or 'the market' must be mediated. Political and social organisation that sets individuals up alone against states and markets can have negative effects, both on individuals and on the wider society.

Our third premise follows from the previous two. People on the ground should be involved collectively in policy making that affects their area of work or habitation; they should be involved in the continuing design and construction of that area; and they should be involved in its maintenance.

These are premises. They are not directly argued for here. Rather, they themselves are the outcome of decades of argument in public policy, ethics and political theory on the subjects of states, markets and communities (Frazer 1999; Gray 1993). However, we also start with the observation that attempts to 'empower communities', 'consult local people', 'regenerate neighbourhoods' and the like have frequently been disappointing for a number of reasons. Among these are:

- the insufficient resources allowed for maintenance of capital projects;

- the capacity of corporate power to maintain an upper hand even where local and national government intentions are opposed to this;

- imbalance between the political efforts put in and the economic and cultural forces at work;

- the lack of effective inclusion of local people and stakeholders in policy design and implementation (Frazer 1999).

This paper elaborates on the third and fourth of these reasons why policy outcomes have been disappointing. It is suggested that policy design and implementation has frequently been based on an insufficiently subtle analysis of *what goods are needed at the local level; why they are needed; in what conditions these goods might be produced; and how they might be distributed.* Although these are on the face of it very simple and obvious questions, in any practical context they will be difficult to answer. The essay aims to sort out some of the complications, point to some possible solutions, and consider some possible policy responses. In particular, I argue that in order to address such questions satisfactorily we need to see how, first, *precise patterns of local social relations can have perverse effects on the production of social goods*; second that *the production and maintenance of different goods rely on particular patterns of local social relations* and third that *shared social goods themselves affect and produce patterns of local social relations, for good or for ill.*

For simplicity's sake I refer to 'patterns of local social relations' as 'local groups and networks'. Desired policy outcomes such as well-maintained public spaces or trusting and civil local behaviour will be described for short as policy 'goods'. The absence of these outcomes will be termed 'lacks', whilst policy problems such as anti-social behaviour or abandoned green spaces will be described as policy 'bads'. Groups and networks on the one hand and goods, lacks and bads on the other are closely connected. In his essay in this volume Perri 6 considers what patterns of social relations policy makers should support and why. Networks can afford groups and individuals a wide range of goods such as opportunities for learning, social support, information and so on. They can equally fail to generate such goods or to provide them where they are currently lacking. And they can even generate policy 'bads' such as the drug-dealing or theft that can arise from local criminal networks. In this paper I am concerned to trace the connection in the opposite direction. Different kinds of policy goods rely on and call for different groups and network patterns if they are to be produced and distributed justly and efficiently. Two important types of good valued at the neighbourhood level will be discussed in this light with a view to establishing what sort of social relations they assume.

Private and communal goods

So far I have used the terms 'goods', 'lacks' and 'bads'. These need further explanation. When we consider the general political project of resolving bads and lacks and provision of goods, of course we can be talking about any of a very wide range of things: roads and streetlights, railways, leisure facilities, education, health, public health, open spaces, laws and norms, shared buildings, residential areas, friendship networks, cultures and 'ways of life', public safety, social clubs, justice and so on. A good deal of both political theory and policy thinking addresses questions about how these various goods should be provided. For convenience we can group this diverse list into four types:

- things that are conventionally now treated as *commodities* (such as food or clothing);

- a specific group of commodities or *durable goods* that are used for production and reproduction (for example, washing machines, garden machinery, print machinery, and we can also include in here technologies for communication and entertainment – TV, video, telephone etc);

- *amenities* such as residential areas, parks and gardens, sports facilities, buildings and spaces for public use;

- more *abstract or act-centred* goods such as security, trust or civility. Although public policy often shies away from discussing these matters, values, norms, cultures and 'ways of life' are really a key political issue in modern societies with all their problems of fragmentation, alienation and exclusion.

These different types of good can be produced and distributed in a variety of ways but the key distinction that we need to think about in this context is whether or not they are to be treated as private or communal. Privately-owned goods give individuals clear rights and responsibilities over their use. With communal goods the matter is rather less clear and as will be seen, this may prove to be a problem (Coleman 1990; Gray 1993; McLean 1987; Olson 1971).

In the era of capitalism politics must decide whether all commodities should be left to the market to supply. Is there a case for governmental distribution of some commodities (for example, giving poor people food stamps instead of cash benefits)? What, if anything, should be shared among residents in a locality (a local launderette or a bath house)? Although we may think that questions of whether goods should be publicly or privately provided are really only relevant at the level of national services, this chapter argues that we must address the question of whether the goods that we want at the local level should be communal or private and how, exactly, they should be provided. The goods that we share at the local level may be argued to have important benefits that go beyond the immediate benefit to individual users.

The precepts of the market mean that the concept of sharing goods locally may sound anachronistic; this need not be the case. Although socialists in the West may have given up, more or less, on the idea of public canteens, the ideal of sharing food has a prominent place in multicultural politics, in projects to relieve poverty and so on. 'Community politics' projects have often been focussed around car sharing or bike banks, food co-operatives, or toy libraries. It is, of course, important to remember how much political effort and energy has gone into projects to transform goods that traditionally have been shared (wells, taps, baths and laundries spring to mind) from communal into private goods. At the same time, of course, some goods that traditionally were thought of as private (education, personal healthcare) have been transformed in modern states into public shared goods. These shifts, and continuing controversies about whether goods are or should be public or private, whether and how 'market forces' drive out social provision, and how social provision can compensate for market failure, alert us to the fact that the status of goods (private, communal, public) is almost always a *political* matter.

In the present political context several reasons can be suggested why goods that often are thought of as ideally *private* should be thought of instead as *communal*.

- The *efficiency argument* in these contexts emphasises the waste from privatisation: especially of non-renewable energy sources, but also waste from sub-optimal use of, say, machinery (garden machinery, laundry equipment are examples) or space (gardens, swimming pools). If such goods are shared by the individuals living in a particular area or building that makes for a more efficient use of space, energy and maintenance effort than if each household purchases, houses and uses their own.

- The *sociability argument* emphasises that sharing machinery, facilities, and spaces means that people will interact with each other more. In a world where isolation and loneliness are real social problems with social costs (not just costs to the isolated and lonely individuals) then organisations and institutions than encourage sharing and sociability are very valuable.

- The *justice argument* emphasises that sharing gives people who otherwise would not have it access to goods. Some people can afford to buy their own washing machine or swimming pool; others cannot. The institution of sharing means that individuals are not deprived of useful and necessary goods because of poverty.

● The *symbolism argument* emphasises that sharing arrangements have a symbolic value, independent of their justice or efficiency values. The organisation of sharing, everyone making their contribution and everyone taking out their benefit, in whatever field, symbolises solidarity, mutuality and co-operation. This argument seems to be very important in contemporary community politics – especially when projects and shared resources are beleaguered or threatened. People are reluctant to see shared goods go, not just because the loss of a swimming pool or clinic or tool-sharing scheme is the loss of an amenity or service but because of what the loss symbolises. Losses like these symbolise the loss of community and solidarity, they symbolise individualism and fragmentation.

The upshot of these arguments is that even if the rights and responsibilities of private ownership and use are clearer there are many good reasons why some of the goods we value at local level might have to be communal.

Let us now look more closely at the two groups of goods particularly at issue in contemporary political debate about local quality of life. In the case of *public spaces and local amenities* – neighbourhoods, streets, civic centres, parks, play, sport and leisure space – the efficiency argument draws our attention to the fact that it is inconceivable that every household could have their own leisure and sport space. Physically it would be impossible for everyone to have enough if everyone had to have their own. This is quite independent of the actual facts of inequality which mean that although some rich people have considerable amounts of space others have none (certainly, an argument from social justice would recommend communal provision on these grounds). In fact, 'efficiency' doesn't really come close to articulating what is at stake here – which is *necessity*. Even in a society which values privacy and private property above all else, it would be absolutely necessary that there be shared pavements and roadways to afford access to private property. In this sense privacy depends on sharing. It is not the case then that shared goods are an option in a society of individuals.

But perhaps the more significant arguments about shared space in the current political context are those that focus on *sociability* and the associated modes of conduct *publicness*, *civicness* and *civility*. When relationships and modes of conduct are public it means they are open and visible. When they are civic it means they acknowledge and participate in the ideals of citizenship and local government and administration. When they are civil it means they are appropriate to citizens and fitting with the social aspects of citizenship. When people share a space, and relate to each other in these ways, particular kinds of sociability are implied. In particular, these involve recognising the relationship between the social interactions that go on between strangers, neighbours and kin, friends and antagonists, and the political institutions and authority that have constructed the public space in which these interactions are conducted.

Our attention here is also drawn to the *symbolism* argument in connection with ways of life and with amenities. Even if shared spaces don't actually embody the civic, civil and public ideals of visibility, citizenship, sociability and political power, at least they symbolise them, or rather perhaps symbolise our aspiration to the realisation of these ideals. Of course in reality shared spaces such as streets or parks can feature fights, intimidation, economic and personal coercion, insults, abuse, exploitation and oppression. The point of talking about the symbolism of civility and the rest is not an idealistic starry-eyed view of public spaces. Rather the point is that those individuals and groups who oppose those undesirable outcomes – who attempt to stop abusive behaviour, attempt to reclaim the night, or whatever – can point to the ideals of shared public life that involve free and equal access, the right to be unmolested, treated civilly and with respect. They can argue, validly, that abusive, coercive, oppressive behaviour *should not occur*. Furthermore the meaning of 'public' involves our interest in other people's conduct, and our share in public goods involves our right and responsibility to defend them. Public space, as such, symbolises civil values and that lends power to demands that the conduct of all, in this space, should accord with those values.

Let us now turn to *values*, *norms*, and *ways of life* themselves. Some norms, values, or ways of life can be thought of straightforwardly as private goods. In a number of systems and traditions of political thought the idea that 'it's up to the individual himself to decide what he believes and how he behaves' is commonplace and can be interpreted as though beliefs and behaviours 'belong' just to the individual. However, a good deal of communitarian writing and community politics is focussed on the perceived dangers of this tendency. There is concern that it has damaging social consequences such as fragmentation, alienation, the loss of mutuality, co-operation and social support. For if people's values and modes of conduct are just their own then we lack a stable basis for predicting how others are going to behave and thereby we lack security. Further, some versions of this model imply there should be no constraint on choice of values and modes of conduct. Together with the view that 'it is just up the individual to decide' this means that we can lack moral or political resources to limit or criticise modes of conduct that are offensive, insulting, disorderly or harmful. On these grounds, it is argued that values, norms and ways of life must be, and be thought of, as communal rather than private goods.

From the point of view of community politics, shared values have tremendous capital advantages. If at least some basic values are shared communication is easier. If people believe they understand others' preferences then they can act more freely. On the other hand it is a mistake to presume that all values must be shared for effective local relationships and social networks to operate; and it can be a great mistake to emphasise the 'values we all share' over the 'variations among us'. To argue that values, ways of life and commitment to modes of conduct should be shared is by no means to imply that it could ever finally be settled exactly what counts, for instance, as 'civility'. To take a couple of contemporary examples, for some eating in the street or hanging out in public spaces are on the border of the uncivil or even perceived straightforwardly as disorderly and antisocial. Such examples make clear that the sense in which a 'way of life' or 'modes of conduct' might be shared is one in which citizens are able to accept that conduct in public affects other people and can be constrained as such. This also implies that ways of life and modes of conduct are the proper subject of political debate, and that politics being what it is, as new groups and generations enter the polity, and new technologies and material conditions emerge, standards of conduct and behaviour in public life will change.

Summary

As these pages show there are several politically salient arguments why certain goods – some commodities, some forms of technology, some spaces and amenities, and some values and aspects of ways of life – should be *communal* and shared rather than *private*. Negative consequences can follow from the solely private provision and consumption of such goods, and also from their absence. Where these policy 'goods' such as shared public spaces and local amenities, common ways of life and values are lacking policy 'bads' such as urban and rural decay, crime and anti-social behaviour can fill the gap. The next section will show why it is so important that policy-makers think about the type of local social relations required to support valued local goods that are supposed to be communal and shared.

The power of the commons

When goods are common they bring two kinds of benefits. First they bring privately enjoyable benefits to individuals. Second they bring common benefits to all who use them. Individuals get to eat a plate of food, use a decent lawnmower, practise their swimming, or move freely and securely about a public space. But the common benefits extend far beyond these individual satisfactions. In sharing we are and must be aware of others, aware of our relations with others, and have a sense of one's own good as tied up with the good of others.

The idea of *the commons* then is a continuing potent political ideal. Conveying less rhetorical baggage than the ideal of 'community' it clearly has a straightforward material and concrete reference – what we all share, and what we all stand to lose. First, the idea is that there are some goods we simply can't have 'privately' or 'individually'. Access to our private property is one of the most prominent. Security and safety in public spaces is another. Shared amenities that meet conditions of efficiency and justice are further goods of the commons. Second, there is the intriguing idea that sharing does not diminish, but augments, some goods. Most goods diminish with use, and diminish even faster if they are shared (a plate of food, for example). But some goods – friendship, trust, civility – *seem to increase in quantity with use rather than diminish.* Trust builds trust. Friendship builds friendship. Civility builds civility (Gambetta 1988).

Here the idea of *social capital* is salient (Coleman 1988). The point of 'capital' is that it is a good which generates a return with interest. Financial capital, when invested, attracts financial interest or a return. Social capital, when invested, attracts a social interest or return. So exercising friendship or trust in others will attract a return in the form of more friendship or trust, or more of some other social good like social support or co-operation.

However, just as the consumption and production of some goods can get into this kind of virtuous spiral, so the consumption and destruction of goods can get into a vicious spiral. In some contexts, the very robust social goods that augment with use can look more like very fragile goods that diminish at a rate faster than individuals get satisfaction from them.

Tragedies of the commons

The problem with common goods is that they often are not cared for as well as private goods are. Shared kitchens tend to be dirtier, on average, than private kitchens; shared gardens and open spaces can be litter strewn and ill-kempt while private gardens are, on average, neat and pretty. In severe cases common goods can be destroyed. Streams and canals fill up with rubbish. Open spaces are strewn with glass and dog dirt. Children's playgrounds rust and crack. These are, of course, the images of the 'urban wasteland' or the 'rural dump'. Another term for this is the *tragedy of the commons* (Gray 1993; McLean 1987).

The 'tragedy' of the commons is this. Given the classic example of common grazing land, we can see that if others are grazing their animals then, from the point of view of any individual, he might as well too. Otherwise he is suffering *more* than others, disadvantaging himself whilst not reducing the harm done by any significant amount. On the other hand, supposing the parties reach an agreement that everyone will restrict their grazing to maintain the land, then it really does make sense for at least somebody to free ride. The problem is that the same reasoning applies to everyone. If everyone independently comes to the conclusion that it doesn't matter if *they* don't do *their* bit because the others will do theirs, then the result is *nobody* doing their bit. This is the tragedy of the commons, and it is this problem of co-ordination and absence of clear responsibility which explains why many of our urban spaces are currently in a state of decay.

We need to know how this problem can be addressed: what options are available to policy-makers who wish to ensure that the quality of the goods we use and share at local level is maintained or improved? There are several possible responses and each may have different expectations of and impact upon local social relations. Only if we understand this can a solution appropriate to the area be found. Invoking the example of a community garden some options would include:

- The local residents currently making an effort might become pure altruists, and maintain the garden, amenity or public space for everyone's enjoyment.

- The residents currently making an effort might stop doing so – because they don't like being made 'mugs' while others shirk, or because the combined non-efforts of the shirkers ruins their work. In this case the garden, street or public space goes to rack and ruin; the common good is spoiled.

- Alternatively, the whole group, whether currently making an effort or not, could be encouraged to see the way of 'enlightened self interest' and organise itself so that shirking, free riding, and cheating either are not possible or if possible are effectively 'punished'. Community development work and local regeneration projects may help to achieve these aims. Without such help, this may be possible in small groups, close-knit societies, areas where close surveillance is possible and part of the culture or where norms are powerful and powerfully enforced.

- The group might hand over responsibility to an authority independent of the group itself such as the local authority or a private security firm. The authority polices and enforces. An example of this response might be the policing of the area by paid Neighbourhood Wardens. (A more familiar example is the 'privatisation' of shopping malls where previously public space is policed by hired security.)

- Perhaps the most familiar political way for the tragedy of the commons to be addressed is by the authoritative provision of *public goods*. In the theory of orthodox economics public goods are universal or non-excludable (if I get light from a streetlight then so does everyone else). They are non-divisible (we can't divide streetlight up some for me some for you) and they are non-rival (my having light doesn't prevent anyone else having light). A public good is one whose consumption and production are both public affairs. Because of the 'free-rider problem' described earlier these goods will not be supplied unless either the people involved can achieve high and stable levels of co-operation and commitment, or a public authority or government oversees production. An example of this approach would be where the local authority decides to provide a local park and park-keepers.

- A final option is for residents to provide and maintain the facilities or spaces as club goods. In this scenario, some local residents may be happy to keep maintaining the quality of local facilities or spaces but are likely to be unhappy about sharing the results of their efforts with the shirkers. So the people putting in the work may take steps to secure what was a truly common good just for themselves. In this case it is no longer a common good, but has become a club good. It is shared just between those people who are members of the club that exists to enjoy the good. An example of this approach would be the many private parks and gardens to be found in the centre of London's residential squares.

Although not usually a feature of discussions about how to regenerate deprived areas such talk of public, private and club goods is important because it focuses attention on what is required for policy outcomes (such as clean streets, pleasant parks, low car use and so on) to be maintained in the future. It forces us to think about the incentives or disincentives, and the types of relationship that have to be in place for these valued local goods to be preserved. The conclusion to be drawn from the options laid out above is that unless local social relations can be altered to become more trusting and altruistic, the quality of the local environment and facilities will not be maintained without either state intervention and provision or restriction of the goods to local 'clubs' of residents. Any policy decision must realistically face up to this challenge.

Another reason for focusing on the implications of these different options is that it also enables us to identify the likely impact on 'sharing'. At least one of these options clearly leads to a scenario where the use of the good, or community garden in this case, is limited to only some community members. This conflicts with the earlier arguments put forward to reveal the importance of sharing certain goods in common at local level. It is worth noting though that even government provision of the goods as 'public goods' may not avoid this outcome. A characteristic of public goods, proper, is that they are non-rival. My benefiting from street lighting doesn't prevent others benefiting. For some goods it really is true that their benefit is not subject to congestion or to crowding. (Hirsch 1976) For most goods, though, common sense tells us this is not true. A single streetlight, even a street full of lights, is certainly subject to crowding. Certain individuals under certain conditions would not benefit from it because they can't get physically near enough. This could be because the street is 'full' so to speak; or it could be because some people are discouraged or even prevented from using certain streets – by the dominance of certain social groups, or physical barriers, or transport patterns. This may not seem so important if we are talking about street lights but could be more of an issue if the good at stake is a park, medical centre or community centre.

Another way of thinking about these goods (clean air, pleasant living environments, public amenities) is as *positional goods* and it is important to identify who is unable to access them and why. They fall, morally speaking, into two kinds. First some goods are *fragile*, in the sense of subject to destruction by crowding. A 'better view' got in a theatre or stadium by standing up is destroyed once everyone stands up. Lovely views, clean air, and peace and quiet in some residential locations are certainly vulnerable to crowding: all these things can disappear as more and more people move in to share them. Second, though some goods are *exclusive goods*. In some cases the whole point of a certain good is that *others can't have it*. In the case of a good school, or any good neighbourhood, it can be the case that part of the value is that not everyone, or not all types of people, have access to it. There are then incentives for current residents of the neighbourhood or current school parents to ensure that 'less desirable' groups cannot enter or join.

This raises issues about exclusion on a level that goes beyond current policy concerns for social inclusion. Policy innovations that are themselves defended on the grounds of 'community power' – such as increased parental involvement in schools, tenants' control over housing and so on – can have just this kind of exclusive outcome. So also can league tables which increase the incentives for schools and other institutions to discourage clients who are likely to cause problems or make targets harder to achieve.

Summary

The story so far has traced a line from the desirability of communal goods such as clean streets and pleasant green spaces, via problems with their provision and the outright 'tragedy of the commons', to a range of possible solutions. Some of these solutions seem to undermine the possibility of those local goods being genuinely shared whilst others make unrealistic expectations of local social relations. Policy-makers must address these concerns to ensure that local services and goods are provided in a way which is genuinely sensitive to the expectations of and impact upon local social relations.

Localities: Boundaries and relationships

As we have seen, shared local amenities and spaces are closely tied up with public security (Crawford 1998). If the quality of shared spaces and amenities decline, confidence in the public space and local willingness to protect it will also decline, and with that the reasonable expectation of civil conduct. The policy problem we face then is how to make sure that shared goods – the commons – are provided and maintained. We argue that accurate and sophisticated understanding of the nature of social relationships in the locality is a necessary first step towards the satisfactory provision of these goods. There are several connected issues which policy-makers need to address in order to ensure appropriate provision but which are currently ignored.

The first problem that policy makers (and I take it throughout this paper that the category 'policy makers' must include local people) face is that despite the current confident policy focus on 'neighbourhoods' the *shape of the relevant social and spatial area* is rarely obvious (Frazer 1999). *First*, there is an individual subjective element to it. Different individuals have different views about where the boundaries of an area lie, who is included and who lies beyond the boundaries of some social group. These individual judgements, of course, vary with the individual's own life experience, daily routine, and so on. *Second* there is a politically constructed element to it: local authorities, health authorities, social services departments, all identify discrete 'areas' not all of which will coincide. These in turn may fail to coincide with people's personal perceptions of 'their area'. *Third* there is a value construction also. Some areas are labelled as 'good' or 'bad'. People who live in 'bad' areas often engage in attempts to re-value their area – this is the stuff of traditional community politics.

Any of these social and mental 'maps' of an area can be quite inappropriate to a policy issue, misleading as to 'sociological reality' or both. Quite simple studies of patterns of geographical movement can change the way policy makers view an issue – for example, there might be cases where policy makers assume that a particular transport route is needed while people in the area are oriented in a different direction. The provision of goods and resources in one locale may be of less use to local people and visitors than the provision of the same goods elsewhere.

There is, however, a further *ideological problem* which is not straightforwardly soluble by mapping. There are two distinct ways of looking at 'areas' and what they should be and it is not clear that public policy differentiates between them. First, there is the *ideal of the enclave* (Walzer 1983). In an enclave safety and security of those within is secured by quite clear spatial boundaries which also double, of course, as social boundaries. In an enclave resources need to be concentrated inside, usually towards the centre so that inhabitants and members, wherever in the space they are located, have more or less uniform distances to go – to shops and businesses, public spaces and buildings, health services, governmental offices, and so on. This model has often guided the planning of housing estates.

However, the arrangement has a number of disadvantages. First, the enclave model means that outsiders will never 'pass through' and will rarely visit. Although some 'neighbourhood watch' type models of safety see passing strangers as a threat, and therefore this aspect of enclave life as a strength, for the most part it can be argued convincingly that public life, passing traffic, the entry and exit of strangers, and a general sense of public activity, is a greater disincentive to certain kinds of crime and disorder, a greater assurance of safety, and certainly a greater draw for resources (especially but not only commercial trade) than the relatively closed and restricted enclave. In an enclave, residents can be trapped. Enclave perimeters can be barriers to news and communication, especially news and communication about jobs, markets and cultural events. Of course, transport patterns can be a materially powerful factor here – if buses and taxis are few and far between and there are few alternatives, that can increase residents' inwardness. Major roads also form physical barriers to pedestrians, bikes or skates.

The alternative is the *overlapping intermingling of localities* model (Frazer 1999). If resources are at the edges they will be used by residents of more than one locality. If layout is such that travellers pass through on foot or by car or public transport then businesses can generate and exploit passing trade. This model can facilitate the flow of news and information and opportunity – by increasing the range of 'weak ties' (Granovetter 1973;1982). In the enclave model, individuals' ties to others in other localities are likely to be based on kinship or close friendship, or possibly on work. In the overlapping localities model there are likely to be more ties to acquaintances, recognised (but perhaps not intimately known) others. Resources located on the perimeter can carry information that will be picked up by people from more than one locality.

These points shade into a more detailed analysis of networks, dealt with in Chapter 2. They also shade into the second question that policy-makers must address prior to any policy design let alone implementation – that of the *texture of the social and built environment* and the relationship between this and people's networks and lives. We can begin with utilitarian questions about how much and what quality of use various sections of relevant populations get from buildings; the extent to which buildings are single- or multi-use, publicly accessible and usable or monopolised. It is important to emphasise that some policy problems may call for sole use of a building by some enterprise or organisation; others may call for shared use. Where there is sole use – a single organisation or section of the population using a building or space – there can be obvious payoffs in terms of efficiency in the organisation, and density of social relations between the organisation, customers, clients, suppliers and so on. This density can generate positive externalities (external that is to the main business of the organisation in the building). For example, these could include an enhanced service to the locality, enhanced identity in the locality and the ability to participate; a cared-for building and space and so on. But such density may be less beneficial than the looser patterns of ties that result from sharing a space between several organisations and activities as is recognised in the currently-favoured principles of mixed use development.

The third major issue which policy-makers must address is the way political power flows in and around any social and spatial locale. The experience of decades of 'community politics' and 'community initiatives' is that the questions 'who can decide' and 'who can enforce' or execute decisions are the key questions. There are numerous examples of 'consultation', 'decision making forums', 'representation' and so on which are really mechanisms for the neutralisation or dissolution of interests, or are straightforwardly bogus, or ineffective. On the other hand, there are also examples of local people being given control of real resources (real money) to deploy on local projects in an institutional set-up which ensures that salient social groups and proto-groups (the young, the old, parents, sports players, others) have an appropriate say.

For this to happen there must be adequate local sociological knowledge of who the salient groups and networks are. Furthermore, this mapping of networks must be sensitive to those networks and groups that are 'latent', not yet formed. A good model for mapping networks is youth, actually. Young people form groups, knots and networks, usually around some activity or focal point. These groups are shifting and frequently short-lived; they can seem disorganised and aimless. Yet, during the time of their activity, these are groups who must have a say in the locale they inhabit, and must be engaged in addressing the nature of the social relationships and dilemmas they generate. Too often these groups are seen simply as threatening and disorderly. Frequently, there is focus on the disruption and danger attributed to them – and to be sure, young people can generate noise and mess, and can, of course, be involved in risky or dangerous activities. But the other positive way of looking at this is that they are generating energy. Furthermore, these groups are dynamic. And they go, as quickly as they come.

Traditionally, 'politics' has focussed on *stable groups* such as organised parties, social clubs and relatively fixed interests. Such stable groups are often the holders of valuable resources for organisation, or communication, or administration. But these stable groups are most often exclusive and exclusionary or relatively difficult to join. So using them as the repositories for political power – seeking consultation there, or recruiting 'representatives' or working party members – can fail to have the desired wide participatory and legitimising effects that are sought. 'Disorganised' groups often have their legitimacy questioned. They are said to be 'unrepresentative'. However, I argue we need to flip this reasoning on its head. *Disorganised groups* are generators of energy. They may not last long, but while they last they have social resources, motivations, engagement and intelligence (in both senses of that word). As such they must certainly be involved or consulted along with other more stable groups.

Of course, the provision of budgets means that there has to be a stable bureaucracy to maintain continuity. Crucially too, the provision of shared goods involves continued commitment to maintenance. Too many playgrounds, gardens, shared buildings, or events are funded without funding the continued provision of caretakers, maintenance staff or fundraisers for the next stage: all the things that are needed if cycles of decline are to be avoided. But the permanent or semi-permanent organisation must, month on month, be aware of who is in the locale, constantly drawing on ephemeral groups that come and go, generating energy.

Summary

This section has argued that as well as attending to the details of local social relations policy-makers must also take three key issues into account when deciding how to appropriately supply valued local goods such as leisure facilities, local amenities or green spaces. Of particular importance is the need to focus on disorganised groups as well as organised ones. However, even if these considerations are taken into account, the earlier analysis of the logic of shared and public goods showed how easy it is for these valuable goods to become 'club goods'. We now to look more closely at 'clubs', and explore their possible relationship with the kind of loose networks here identified as important for healthy local social relations and provision.

The dangers of club goods

One aim of this essay is to consider two groups of goods that in many contexts need to be held in common at the local level and to consider the issues that surround their provision. We have considered firstly a range of public amenities such as open spaces, shared buildings, sports and leisure facilities, pleasant and safe public spaces; and secondly the more abstract goods that are closely linked to these amenities: a culture of civility, safety, mutual trust and reciprocity, in short a public, democratic and civil culture. It was suggested that one of the reasons why a policy focus on community is valuable is because it forces us to consider what we share at the local level and why such sharing is important, as well as how it can be sustained. In the first section of this chapter we put aside the possibility of a just, efficient, or sociable world in which these goods are thought of as wholly private. We may also have grounds for doubt about the practicality or efficacy of their provision as public goods by central or even local government – on grounds of inefficiency, and the need for these goods to be 'owned' at a more local level. But the ideal of the 'small, close-knit community' in which everyone pulls their weight and shares what little they have, needs to be more settled and stable and requires higher levels of surveillance and conformity than modern conditions will allow. In any case, the logic of the 'tragedy of the commons' emphasises that the resolution will often be found in 'clubs' – in people who are both willing to contribute and anxious to benefit from the production and distribution of some good, coming together in such a way as to exclude shirkers and cheats. This is not an obviously attractive solution.

The first problem that arises is the question of how club membership is to be secured. As a solution to the tragedy of the commons, the exclusion of shirkers and cheats may well be ethically justified. The 'club' is a *club of contributors*. However, as we have seen, 'clubs' can when looked at from the outside look more like a corruption of public goods. The question of how one becomes a member is pressing. In many cases the answer seems to be that these are *clubs of those who can monopolise and exclude*. It is unfortunately not the case, for example, that the only qualification required for all residents' associations is that of residing in the neighbourhood.

By the same token, there are other groups of people who constitute clubs of the dispossessed. The logic that means that ostensibly public or common goods actually accrue to limited and bounded clubs also means that what ought to be public bads and lacks accrue to limited and bounded clubs also. In this way certain groups in a locality can suffer disproportionately – young people or the elderly may often suffer most from the failure to provide certain leisure facilities for example. Undoubtedly some club goods can generate positive externalities so that other social groups or even the public at large enjoy by-products of the goods enjoyed by club members. By the same token, the negative externalities generated from the circulation of bads among deprived groups will be felt by the wider public or sections of it. Complaints of anti-social or intimidating behaviour by bored adolescents can affect a wide circle of local residents, even though the direct cause of this behaviour could just be the lack of facilities for a small group of youngsters.

Three points must be picked up from this. *First* club goods can in some cases be taken to be an acceptable or even a preferable substitute for difficult efforts to provide and distribute genuine public goods especially where government resources are scarce. But, justice demands that we recognise and deal with the fact that club goods rely on exclusion. The *second* implication of this is that bad outcomes and lack of resources are distributed 'lumpily'. In some groups policy bads (such as drugs or anti-social values) circulate, or they may lack key resources and the group will bear nearly all the costs of these itself. I say 'nearly all' because the *third* and most important point is that externalities of bads and lacks, like externalities of goods, spill over to other groups and into the wider population.

We can easily think of cases where the failure of provision of club goods (lacks) or the production of 'club bads' not only makes the club members suffer, but also generates externalities that negatively affect members of the wider public. If young people living on a particular estate lack resources like activity centres, education, jobs and so on, this has widespread effects. Thus, it might be thought, this wider public has an intrinsic interest in these particular young people being resourced. Certainly it is the instinct of *justice* theorists that the proper response to deprivation is provision and compensation. But it is also important to note an alternative political and moral response which stems not from a concern with justice but from a concern with *social order*. This concern suggests and enables another possible way of dealing with the situation.

This unattractive but effective option is *containment* which would ensure the group's lack of resources does not affect others. The group can be separated geographically, made invisible, and marginalised and disempowered to the extent that they no longer affect others. So the 'wider public' can protect itself from the effects of deprivation. Low public transport provision to and from certain housing locales can work to confine ill-resourced people. The externalities generated by such a group will then be felt mainly or only in their immediate neighbourhood. Although effective, containment is clearly a highly undesirable policy option, reinforcing both the extent and visibility of social exclusion.

Summary

So far, this chapter has made the following key points:

- Precise patterns of local social relations can have perverse effects on the production and maintenance of important social goods such as public spaces, clean streets or local amenities. In particular, different levels of commitment to the neighbourhood can bring about a 'tragedy of the commons' scenario whereby social goods aren't produced at all, or are produced and maintained by clubs of contributors who will take steps to exclude non-contributors. This can result in 'clubs of the dispossessed' and a resulting culture of antagonism, protectiveness and exclusion in a locality.

- Conversely, the production and maintenance of different social goods relies on particular patterns of social relations. It may be fine for 'clubs' of parents of under-fives to police a small children's playground – the degree of exclusivity thus constituted may be an ethical and socially desirable solution to the problem of the maintenance of common goods. But supposedly public buildings or spaces can be unacceptably monopolised by particular groups and networks. The good of civility and genuine public life requires access for all. Somehow this access has to be secured.

- Similarly, lacks and bads – poverty of resources, risky environments, harmful behaviour and actions – can be spatially and socially confined to particular groups or people in particular bounded areas. One solution to the problem of the negative externalities generated by a particular group or network or people in a locale is to sequester them – to erect barriers over which the negative externalities can't spill. Equally, such a barrier also means that the positive externalities from neighbouring groups, networks and locales don't aid the dispossessed people.

Conclusions

Where does all this leave the project of 'reclaiming community'? Several important conclusions can be drawn from the foregoing discussion which have implications across a range of policy areas, but which hold specific relevance for regeneration and urban policy.

First, everything points to the importance of shared amenities – safe public streets, pleasant open spaces, plenty of sports and leisure facilities, useful and public buildings. In particular this is required to support the minimal sharing of common values at least as those define what is acceptable 'public' behaviour.

Second, the needs that have to be met, and the design and location of the amenities, can only be properly diagnosed and understood with appropriate consultation and involvement of interested parties. The argument of this essay is that consultation should not just be with established and organised groups, but that attention must also be paid to disorganised and even disorderly networks, as well as isolated individuals.

Third, the temptation to locate all amenities at the centres of enclaves should be resisted. From the point of view of civic values and democratic politics it is far preferable for locales to flow into one another and mingle rather than being clearly bounded. Obviously the clustering of amenities (swimming pool, park) has benefits and so does the combination of 'civic amenities' and commercial enterprises.

Fourth, 'clubs' of residents using and maintaining amenities and spaces can be an ethical and politically helpful solution to the tragedy of the commons. However, the identification of any space or amenity with particular people, groups or networks can repel others. In this case, civic values are not being maintained or symbolised.

Fifth, steps must be taken to ensure that public goods are truly public. Some goods must be supplied and maintained by authorities regardless of who contributes to them, who uses them, even who damages them. Throwing money at public goods is quite a good strategy. In order to act out and symbolise civic values litter and broken glass must be picked up from streets, parks, and indeed everywhere else, and refuse collected as often as needed. From high density housing areas or high use public areas this will certainly be more often than is the practice in most locales. A problem has been that local and national authorities are often neglectful and inefficient. Litter-strewn play areas, dilapidated sports facilities, dumping and so on are just the most visible signs of this.

Sixth, 'neglect' and 'inefficiency' in governmental agencies can, however, also be seen as yet another sign of a more general disintegration of political culture, and, especially, civic culture. The ideals of civic life mean very little to very many people, including influential individuals in powerful positions. That refuse collection symbolises political power and civic values is an idea that is lost on citizens, officials and government employees alike who are inclined to see it more simply as a necessary material service which is costly to deliver.

So, *finally*, this difficult problem of political culture also needs to be addressed. Clearly arguments from social justice against exclusion must be made vigorously. They must be joined with these arguments about the complex relationships between shared goods and patterns of local social relationships, about 'the commons' and what it enables and what it symbolises in civic life.

References

Blau P (1964) *Exchange and Power in Social Life* New York: Wiley

Coleman J (1988) 'Social Capital in the Creation of Human Capital' *American Journal of Sociology* 94 (supplement)

Coleman J (1990) *Foundations of Social Theory* Cambridge, Mass: Harvard University Press

Crawford A (1998) *Crime Prevention and Community Safety: politics, policies and practices* London: Longman

Frazer E (1999) *The Problem with Communitarian Politics: unity and conflict* Oxford: Oxford University Press

Gambetta D (ed) (1988) *Trust: making and breaking cooperative relations* Cambridge: Cambridge University Press

Granovetter M (1973) 'The Strength of Weak Ties' *American Journal of Sociology* 78

Granovetter M (1982) 'The Strength of Weak Ties: a Network Theory Revisited' in Marsden P V and Lin N (eds) *Social Structure and Network Analysis* Beverly Hills: Sage Publications

Gray J (1993) *Beyond the New Right: markets, government and the common environment* London: Routledge

Hirsch F (1976) *Social Limits to Growth* Cambridge Mass.: Harvard University Press

Hirschman A (1970) *Exit, Voice and Loyalty: Responses to Decline in Firms, Organisations and States* Cambridge, Mass: Harvard University Press

McLean I (1987) *Public Choice: an introduction* Oxford: Basil Blackwell

Olson M (1971) *The Logic of Collective Action: public goods and the theory of groups* 2nd edition, Cambridge, Mass.: Harvard University Press

Schelling T (1978) *Micromotives and Macrobehaviour* New York: Norton

Walzer M (1983) *Spheres of Justice* New York: Basic Books

Young IM (1990) *Justice and the Politics of Difference* Princeton: Princeton University Press

III: Policy and practice so far

4. Neighbourhood regeneration policy: rebuilding community?

Robina Goodlad

This essay argues that current British policy on neighbourhood regeneration is strengthened by its focus on community and that this experience has relevance to policy making in other spheres, with lessons about what public policy should avoid as well as what it might attempt. The chapter starts by discussing the issues that are raised by bringing the concept of community side by side with the concept of neighbourhood. It then considers how 'community' has played a role in neighbourhood regeneration, concentrating particularly on citizen involvement in neighbourhood governance, and finally considers what lessons have emerged for regeneration practice and for other policy fields.

Community and neighbourhood in social science and public policy

Several important strands in current neighbourhood regeneration policy can be seen as having their origins in social science concerns with community. 'We are it seems at another peak of interest in issues of neighbourhood and community... The labels may have changed but the essential questions have not' (Forrest and Kearns 2001). These 'essential questions' are concerned with how people relate to each other within neighbourhoods after the social and economic changes of the last 20 years. What is the significance of community and neighbourhood amongst other factors in determining or constraining life chances and personal identities? Is the significance of neighbourhood social relationships greater for some people than others? Is a sense of community in a neighbourhood setting being replaced or complemented by ties that bind people in other networks or in cyberspace? How should public policy for neighbourhoods take account of popular attachment to the concept of community and the widespread fear of its loss?

The relationship between social relations and place has been the subject of intense debate in urban studies, social geography and sociology for many years for good practical as well as theoretical reasons. The origins of this concern lay in the industrialisation and urbanisation processes of 19th and early 20th century Britain and America (Hoggett 1997). The resulting literature offers a useful route into considering interconnections between neighbourhood and social relations on one side and the effects of global, national and regional or urban change on the other. A recurring theme since Tönnies wrote about 'gemeinschaft' in the 1880s is the perception that community is not what it used to be and requires rebuilding. Community has been said to be imperilled by migration, disruption to rural patterns of life, high-density living and social, economic and technological change such as participation by women in the labour market, the invention of television and the alleged atomising effects of the internet, the latest source of moral panic (Katz *et al*, 2001). A key question is therefore whether changes originating outside neighbourhoods render irrelevant a policy concern with social relations within neighbourhoods.

It's the economy – and society

Before turning to neighbourhood social relations, we need to acknowledge the contribution of those who engage with the concept of community only to dismiss it as of little importance. The assumption that community is a valuable concept has been challenged, most successfully in the 1980s by sociologists and economic geographers interested in the polarising impact of economic restructuring, which is seen as determining 'locality social systems' more than local factors. The observation that such economic change has had uneven impacts on regions and neighbourhoods continues to generate a stream of area-based analysis in the work of those such as Cooke *et al* (1989) and Turok and Edge (1999). National welfare policy changes have also been analysed to show their impact on social relations at neighbourhood level. For example, the right to buy for council tenants has compounded other processes concentrating the poorest people into the poorest areas so that social rented housing is more heavily concentrated into areas and house types considered less attractive or desirable (Jones and Murie 1999).

This concern with growing social, economic and spatial polarisation, and the increasing sophistication of their analysis, provides one point of departure for policy. It has influenced initiatives such as the establishment of the cross-departmental Neighbourhood Renewal Unit (NRU) within the Department of Transport, Local Government and the Regions in 2001. Economic revival is identified as one of four major themes in the neighbourhood regeneration strategy that drives the work of the Unit (Wallace 2001). A similar concern lies behind the equivalent work of the Scottish Executive, as their social justice policy demonstrates (Scottish Executive 2000).

Neighbourhoods matter too

Useful as they are to understanding the structural causes of social exclusion at small area level, these accounts stressing the impact of economic restructuring, socio-spatial polarisation, welfare change and globalisation neglect the way that social and economic change may interact with every day life or life chances at local level. They underestimate the 'dull routine of everyday life' (Forrest and Kearns 2001) and its role in reproducing social relations and they downplay aspects of neighbourhood conditions such as the concentrations of stigma, crime and poor educational performance that seem to have a compounding effect in interacting with each other in ways that have different outcomes in otherwise similar places. Some social scientists have therefore continued to explore, with policy makers and residents, the notion that the social relations and networks of particular places are distinctive and that they matter to the futures of the areas: 'the idea of community appears to remain alive and well and people, misguidedly or not, continue to refer to it either as something *they live in*, have lost, have just constructed, find oppressive, use as the basis for struggle, and so on' (Hoggett, 1997). From this perspective, the neighbourhood can be seen as a source of resources and social interaction and the base from which people get access to other opportunities and to some aspects of their identity. However, reaching a balanced view on the way that neighbourhood and wider factors interact is very difficult and evidence is partial (see, for example, Buck 2001; Atkinson and Kintrea 2001).

A concern with social relations at neighbourhood level is seen in the remaining three of the four themes of the national strategy for neighbourhood renewal: improving mainstream programmes, developing 'more joined-up local solutions' and seeing neighbourhoods as communities. It 'is essential that neighbourhoods are not seen simply as places, but above all as communities. If neighbourhood renewal is simply "done to" residents, the right solutions will not be found; new funding will simply flow through neighbourhoods rather than enrich the neighbourhood; and residents will be seen as problems not as assets: these are the failures of the many programmes in the past, and that is why community empowerment and involvement are at the heart of the strategy' (Wallace 2001).

Reconnecting neighbourhoods to society

Recent social science writing has moved from observations confined to the nature of social relations in deprived neighbourhoods to explore also links between neighbourhoods and wider society. Although there are many reports of poor neighbourhoods with high levels of internal social cohesion, measured by numbers of friends and relatives in the neighbourhood, for example (see Forrest and Kearns 1999 and Atkinson and Kintrea 2001), a concern has arisen about the consequences that follow from the lower levels of access to wider social networks that people in deprived neighbourhoods are observed to have. Simultaneous high interaction within the area and low interaction with external agencies is seen as problematic. In Putnam's language, this type of 'bonding/getting by' social capital can characterise poor neighbourhoods, whereas the social relationships of middle class people are characterised in addition by 'bridging/getting on' social capital (Putnam 2000).

A concern to bridge the divide between 'disconnected' neighbourhoods and other areas and agencies is a stronger feature of policy for poor neighbourhoods than in the past. The consequences of 'the detachment of poor neighbourhoods' are considered to be serious for regeneration: 'Experience shows that communities thrive best and reinforce their strengths when there are well-established links with other areas and communities. In this way, people come into contact with new opportunities' (SEU, 1998). The origin of this policy approach in social science writing about social capital is apparent. Its strength lies in its recognition of the potential importance of a focus on social relations but its weakness may be a neglect of the social science literature referred to earlier that explores how economic and social forces external to neighbourhoods can lead to differences in the stocks of social capital at neighbourhood level.

It's the individual

Finally, the sociology of identity provides another contribution to the analysis of neighbourhood and community. This has offered a new importance to community in the 1990s, by simultaneously reinstating the concept with reference to a sense of identity, while challenging the assumption of a dominant relationship between community and place in its stress on non-place communities of gender, faith, ethnicity, sexuality, work-place and so on. Policy initiatives have recognised this complex mosaic of overlapping communities of identity. Although the national strategy for neighbourhood renewal (SEU 2001) and Scottish Executive reports sometimes use community as a synonym for neighbourhood and there is some ambiguity about what the word is intended to convey, it is recognised that there are a variety of ways in which manifestations of 'community' can be valued and fostered. The neighbourhood renewal Action Plan, for example, recognises 'communities of interest', 'faith communities', 'community organisations', 'residents', and 'voluntary organisations' as stakeholders. The Policy Action Team set up to engage most closely with 'community' concluded, perhaps understandably: 'there is no single model or definition of community' (PAT 9 1999).

This understanding of community identity can contribute a new subtlety to policy-making for neighbourhood initiatives. It recognises the diversity of individuals' relationships to a particular neighbourhood: 'the meanings people ascribe to places where they live can often not be read off from wider economic and social forces' (Hoggett 1997). In particular, the neighbourhood matters more to some people than to others as a focus for community. Social ties beyond the neighbourhood may be more important, for example, to those who drive a car to work every day and occupy a social world in which the neighbourhood may hardly feature. In contrast, for others, in particular older people, some ethnic minorities, unemployed people, women and children, 'the neighbourhood has heightened importance' (Meegan and Mitchell 2001). In addition, these differences of perception may lead to conflicts within neighbourhoods between those who see their neighbourhood as unchanging and those 'identity groups' who have alternative lifestyles or different ethnic, religious or social origins. Diversity – an attribute valued by some – is one way of describing the social conditions that may lead to such tensions but some residents would see such diversity as a problem. Public policy may have to be concerned then with the implications of the heterogeneity of community identity within a neighbourhood or the tensions associated with interactions between particular groups within neighbourhoods as in Belfast and Bradford, for example.

External forces and internal relationships

To sum up, policy makers concerned with neighbourhood regeneration have usefully selected several alternative perspectives on community offered by a diverse literature although at times the role and implications of 'community' in regeneration policy has sometimes been unclear. Past policy has varied in its assumptions about the extent to which conditions in poor neighbourhoods are the results of external, mainly economic forces, or internal forces, manifested in 'community breakdown', with a current consensus favouring a mixed (third way?) view that both are important. For example, although the value of community is strongly asserted in the work and publications of the Social Exclusion Unit, it is not to the exclusion of other considerations.

The current approach recognises the interactions between external factors and social relations, while arguing strongly that conditions at local level can be improved with sustained and determined effort. Although community is seen as something that can 'break down' with deleterious effects on anti-social behaviour, crime and so on, the SEU's analysis recognises a wide range of economic, social, physical and other factors at play in creating and sustaining the exclusion of some estates and neighbourhoods. Policy-makers are holding a fine balance between a strong focus on 'community' and internal social relations, which is open to accusations of gilding the ghetto, and a fervent concentration on structural or external determinants of deprivation, which is open to criticisms of utopianism or futility.

Community and area regeneration policy

Before considering in greater detail how 'community empowerment and involvement' have been put at the heart of regeneration policy and what we might learn from past experience, the recent and current policy framework are introduced.

'Community' has been invoked in area regeneration policy frequently since the late 1960s, when the first Urban Programme schemes began. Initiatives have included the Community Development Programme, Task Forces, Estate Action, City Challenge, Housing Action Areas, Renewal Areas, Housing Action Trusts and the Single Regeneration Budget. A focus on neighbourhoods has gone hand in hand with housing policy initiatives that have provided a sharp focus for connecting regeneration policy and 'community'. Regeneration policy has though at times focused on regions rather than neighbourhoods, especially in relation to European Objective One, Social Fund or Regional Development Fund monies. Although some of this activity arguably endangers the prospects of benefit for people resident in poor neighbourhoods, it has nevertheless increasingly been delivered with reference to the need to engage community organisations and build community capacity in deprived areas (Duncan and Thomas 2000; Meegan and Mitchell 2001).

The latest regeneration policy initiatives, the National Strategy for Neighbourhood Renewal (SEU, 2001) and Social Inclusion Partnerships (SIPs) (Scottish Executive, 2000) attempt to learn from previous policy. However, two distinctive new features are, first, that they stem from concerted attempts to root out social exclusion (in England and Wales) and to create social justice (in Scotland). Second, they are supported by government commitments to supporting the process by pledging the involvement of the relevant agencies.

Lessons from past experience reflected in the current approaches include the need:

- to respond to perceived poor 'community' relations;

- for a mixed approach dealing with outer, inner, suburban or rural locations;

- for a focus on cross-cutting, multi-functional partnerships in small areas so that problems such as poor housing and health are linked and co-ordinated action through multi-agency approaches is secured;

- for a more comprehensive approach focusing on physical, social and economic measures as appropriate;

- for an appreciation that a sustained effort may be required over many years to improve conditions in the worst areas; and

- for resident involvement rather than mere rhetoric about it.

The Neighbourhood Regeneration Unit (NRU) leads implementation of the neighbourhood renewal action plan in government departments and within 88 local authorities with the worst concentrations of deprivation where 'Local Strategic Partnerships' (LSPs) bring together public, private and voluntary sector service providers with 'the community' and business sectors. The New Deal for Communities (NDC) programme (£1.9 billion over ten years from 1998) provides lessons in 39 pathfinder areas. Residents (often referred to as the 'community') *have* to be involved in finding solutions to problems. The criteria for inclusion in the programme required that 'all bids will need to involve and engage the community – they won't work if they don't' (SEU 1998). 'Government Office action' is now threatened 'if an LSP did not engage with the community appropriately, and does not take sufficient account of community views' (SEU 2001). Community involvement is said to be hard to achieve, requiring 'facilitation', 'participation of community members in sufficient numbers on the LSP' and 'outreach, especially to excluded communities, to make them aware that they have the chance to express their views and directly influence service providers'.

Regeneration policy in Scotland has taken a different though often parallel route from inner-city initiatives in the 1970s through the *New Life for Urban Scotland* partnerships in four outer-estates from the late 1980s to Priority Partnership Areas and 'Regeneration Programmes' in the mid-1990s (Taylor *et al* 2001). The new Labour Government introduced Social Inclusion Partnerships (SIPs) from 1 April 1999. There are 34 traditional 'area based' partnerships and 14 local theme or issue based initiatives intended to assist young people, care-leavers and other groups. The key focus of area SIPs is deprived neighbourhoods within urban areas, but the programme and choice of language – area regeneration – encompass rural areas and small towns too. Regeneration policy is located administratively within Communities Scotland, a new executive agency directly accountable to ministers. Communities Scotland is expected to establish a 'neighbourhood renewal centre' to develop policy and encourage good practice. The SIPs programme is based on familiar principles, such as a co-ordinated, multi-agency approach; community involvement; and a long-term strategy with commitment from local partners. The rhetoric of community empowerment is as strong in the SIPs policy framework as it is in the SEU's approach. SIPs have funds earmarked for surveys and other forms of consultation and participation. In addition, 'community-based' housing organisations are seen as an important instrument for both regeneration and participation, as they have been since the mid-1970s.

Neighbourhood regeneration and community participation

The presence of 'community' in neighbourhood regeneration policy takes several forms. Community involvement is praised and community participation is fostered in new structures and through funding. Policy stresses the role that residents' groups and voluntary organisations as well as individual citizens may play. Community groups are seen as sources of mutual aid or social cohesion, as service providers and as a possible foundation for citizen involvement in governance. Residents and community groups can be seen as playing one of three roles, which in practice can overlap or occur simultaneously and which are not always clearly spelt out:

- participation in framing local strategies, in monitoring how they are implemented and in commenting on or managing local services; 'communities' need to be involved 'both in designing what is to be done and in implementing it' (Social Exclusion Unit 1998).

- participation in voluntary and community organisations for the immediate pleasure and benefit it brings, because of the benefits it can bring to others and because community and voluntary organisations can serve as a mobilising force for other types of participation; community involvement can 'have the triple benefit of getting things done.., fostering community links and building the skills, self-esteem and networks of those who give their time' (SEU 1998); and

- participation in informal social support mechanisms based on family, friendship and neighbourliness.

'Community participation' may therefore carry several meanings. The remainder of this essay is concerned largely with the first of these forms, participation in governance. The discussion is intended to address two types of question. What has the experience of community participation in regeneration taught us about building community and what has it taught us that might be useful in other policy areas? Before proceeding to that discussion, three contextual features of community participation in neighbourhood renewal with implications for building community are introduced:

- *A new democracy*

    Community participation in neighbourhood renewal has developed in a wider context of experimentation with forms of local participatory democracy that are intended to extend democratisation of the state and build 'community' and social capital. Citizen participation beyond the ballot box has become conventional wisdom. Urban policy has been a particular focus and national and local governments equally see it as essential to successful area regeneration. Policy rhetoric is matched by evidence of a general growth of 'community participation' arrangements in Britain (Lowndes *et al* 1998; Goodlad 2001). Many forms of citizen participation occur at neighbourhood level and include tenant management organisations, estate management boards, community-based housing associations, parent-governor involvement in school management, community councils in Scotland and area committees with community representation. The focus in area policy on not 'doing to' residents but doing things *with* them has reflected wider trends in public policy arising from a belief that neither the state nor the market can create socially cohesive and economically successful cities.

- *Partnership*

  Regeneration policy has increasingly reflected and at times led the current trend to use partnerships as a device for co-ordinating policy development and service delivery. In neighbourhood renewal policy, residents are counted amongst several partners. This has led to particular difficulties in the operation of partnerships in which residents' representatives have sometimes struggled to feel they are able to contribute or influence events as well as other partners (Hastings *et al* 1996), though recent experience suggests that practice has improved (Taylor 2000).

- *Factors which affect participation*

  Although diverse, regeneration neighbourhoods demonstrate characteristics usually associated with low levels of civic participation. In particular, certain socio-economic characteristics such as lower educational attainment are associated with being less likely to know one's neighbours and being less likely to join voluntary organisations. Experience of adversities such as poverty or unemployment is associated with lower social trust (Hall 1999). However, levels of participation within neighbourhoods cannot easily be read off from the socio-economic structure since other factors can intervene – such as membership of formal groups and a high level of political interest (Parry *et al* 1992). Studies show that levels of participation vary by locality and that cities can make a difference (Maloney *et al* 2001). Poor neighbourhoods with a history of regeneration activity and funding can be the locus for relatively high levels of activism (Docherty *et al* 2001).

Constraints and opportunities in building community in regeneration

Turning now to how participation has taken place in neighbourhood renewal, a number of studies have shown that there are difficulties with achieving participation and have provided lessons about how community development can be enhanced (or damaged) through participation. The following section draws on a range of writings to consider the process of community involvement in governance, from a typical starting point of seeking funding for regeneration through designing participation structures to the issues raised for community activists and policy makers by the inevitable focus on activists as the key participants on behalf of the community.

The funding process

Typically, from a policymaker's perspective, regeneration initiatives start with funding opportunities. However, residents may not share the enthusiasm of officials for taking part in developing initiatives. There may be a frustrating history of action taken to secure improvements that have left some activists sceptical about whether a new initiative is going to be any more successful than the last. In addition, initiatives from central and local government and from Europe have often required responses to meet funding deadlines that make community involvement difficult or impossible, while funders simultaneously require evidence of such involvement (Duncan and Thomas 2000; Meegan and Mitchell 2001). Two conventional answers to such criticism are, first, that communities need to be involved 'early' and some useful experience has been gained of 'year zero' preparation for new funding programmes (Chanan et al 1999); and, second, that participation should be seen as a continuous process so that some insight is always available to public officials about the priorities and views of residents. The existence of established relationships will certainly assist last-minute consultation and will build on what is already known. However, this is unlikely to work perfectly, since there may be difficulty in sustaining community involvement in the hope that some resources will turn up and in the absence of any progress towards achieving objectives. In addition, the particular circumstances of new funding opportunities might focus residents' minds in new ways, making fresh consultation desirable. So the two approaches – continuous relationship building and year zero consultation – are better seen as complements than alternatives. Yet it is naïve to imagine that community representatives can always be involved in this way given the volatility of government action. There is sometimes a trade-off between full consultation and other imperatives such as securing funding. This could sometimes be made clearer in the rhetoric that encourages participation.

Achieving a shared meaning of 'participation'

Participation in neighbourhood governance can be hampered by disagreements or confusion about what form of participation is being engaged in. For some people, being informed about what is to happen in the neighbourhood is adequate participation. Others will want to be consulted and given an opportunity to have a say before decisions are taken. A few may be content with nothing short of devolved responsibility for a decision or service. Tension can arise when residents hold different views about the nature of the involvement they want; or assume one form of participation is being offered and find that another is what was intended. A related problem is that decision-making is a complex process and involvement by residents' representatives on one committee or at one set of meetings will not guarantee that they will be present at the crucial stage when decisions are taken. Discussions seeking to resolve such difficulties often take the form of debates about the correct structure, method or technique for participation instead of considering the purposes or processes that participation structures are intended to engender. The focus should be on both the structure for participation and with what actually takes place within that structure. This would help ensure that the complexity of participation is better appreciated: it is rarely a choice between information sharing, dialogue or control – several forms of participation may take place simultaneously or sequentially.

Structures for participation are important too

Although the form or process of participation cannot be assumed from the structure, the detailed design of structures for participation such as committees is important if it is to lead to meaningful community involvement and shared power. Experience shows that it is possible to design structures and achieve processes that enhance community cohesion and a sense of involvement. Docherty *et al*'s (2001) study, for example, shows that the considerable efforts of officials and politicians over many years in two SIP regeneration areas in Glasgow and Edinburgh to engage citizens in debates have led to residents being more likely to feel that the city council involves them in decision-making than residents in two more middle class neighbourhoods in the same two cities. This study also shows that 'community-based' housing associations have demonstrably provided the sense of inclusion that some regeneration structures lack.

Getting results

Many studies of neighbourhood regeneration have shown that community representatives can feel alienated and frustrated as well as liberated and exhilarated by their experience of participation. A mixed picture of achievement and frustration emerges from studies, in which distrust with the governance process is an outcome for some activists who lose patience with the time things take and sometimes withdraw from structures created to involve them. However, more commonly, activists report some sense of achievement as well as some frustration with progress (Duncan and Thomas 1999; Forrest and Kearns 1999). A crucial determinant of their attitude is the extent to which they feel their involvement is achieving something worthwhile. In Docherty *et al*'s study, a stronger sense of inclusion was associated with a perception that the neighbourhood was getting better. A sense of frustration arose from a feeling that there was no point in taking action to report or complain, since experience in the past had shown it did not achieve anything. This seemed to colour attitudes to the council generally. Housing associations have, in contrast, used considerable levels of public funding to achieve more effective consumerist management styles and methods than local authorities and have achieved higher levels of tenant satisfaction and better quality housing (Clapham *et al* 1995; Goodlad 2000). The carrot of access to investment funds gives way typically to higher levels of continuing tenant participation and tenant satisfaction than in the council sector (Clapham and Kintrea 1992; 2000). Associations often become the base for other community activities, such as community care, job creation, play-schemes, and workspace management.

The role of community groups and activists: representing neighbourhood diversity

The notion of community participation raises questions about how the 'community' is to be represented and what community participation has to do with social relations within the neighbourhood. In a homogenous, stable neighbourhood, a community group would stand a fair chance of enhancing social relations by facilitating contact between residents, on one hand and between them and committee members and officials, on the other. Community activists could be taken to be representative of residents generally. But in regeneration neighbourhoods, community groups are varied in the work they do, the organisational ability they demonstrate, the success they feel they achieve and in the resources available to them. While some are impressive in their ability to organise to campaign or provide services or facilities, others suffer from internal difficulties, have little funding and suffer discontinuities in funding. Community activists as well as elected representatives may be seen as lacking legitimacy in speaking for certain residents. Activists may be invisible to some residents who know little or nothing of their work. Also apparent in some cases are disputes arising from personality or political clashes. As a consequence of these factors, groups can find it difficult to win a reputation for trustworthiness and effectiveness amongst fellow-citizens, especially if residents feel the neighbourhood is not improving. Community groups in poor neighbourhoods may suffer doubly because they have fewer of the resources of funding, relationships and skills that assist them to be effective and because residents may be less trusting of activists than occurs in other areas; for example, Docherty *et al*'s study found that residents of two poor regeneration areas demonstrated lower levels of trust in community activists than residents in two more middle class neighbourhoods. Arising from the difficulties that many community groups encounter, policy has recognised the need for additional support such as the employment of community workers and the provision of funding or other resources. Special attention and resources have been devoted to training and support for participation. For example, the Community Empowerment Fund (£36m over three years) supports community and voluntary sector involvement on Local Strategic Partnerships in the 88 areas involved in the neighbourhood renewal strategy and the SIPs programme in Scotland has involved, *inter alia*, over £1 million for training for all types of SIP partners (not only community participants).

Supplementing the contribution of community groups

Community groups cannot be the only mechanism for community participation in neighbourhood governance. Through no fault of their own in many cases, they cannot always be relied on as a source of information about citizens' concerns and priorities. They have neither the resources nor the capacity to consult everyone on behalf of every public agency with a role in their area, yet public agencies sometimes behave as if they have and complain if they cannot live up to this expectation. Given these limitations, distrust by officials about the representativeness of community activists may well be justified in some cases. More systematic methods are required to check the distribution of views on some issues and more generally from time to time. Policy has not always made this explicit. In addition, community groups are sometimes expected simultaneously somehow to transmit the community's *view* while also reflecting the diversity of their area. It is important for officials to deal with this issue sensitively and if possible in association with groups so that officials do not appear to be casting aspersions on the work and capacity of community groups. Policy has therefore increasingly recognised the diversity of neighbourhoods and the difficulty of representation. Participation methods and structures are less likely to rely only on representation by an elite of community activists and are more likely to complement this with one or both of two approaches:

● surveys and other methods that tap into the diversity of social groups and perceptions within the neighbourhood; and

● reliance on voluntary organisations to survey and analyse residents' opinions.

Sharing power

When community organisations are successful in achieving influence and resources they are open to accusations of parochialism and intolerance from those who fear far-reaching 'community empowerment'. Such a fear is often based on a misinterpretation of what community 'empowerment' might mean. The Scottish community-based housing association case shows that it means shared power. The discretion they have is exercised within boundaries set by the law and by a public regulatory body, Communities Scotland, which also supervises the use of public money granted to them. The role of the state is apparent in their work in a number of ways: through funding their development programmes; through the ombudsman; through a set of legal rights to protect individual housing consumers; and through more general legislation, for example on equal opportunities. The evidence is that they feel the same tensions as local authorities in relation to the balance between individual and community rights, in relation to matters such as succession of tenancy, for example, and that they sometimes reach alternative conclusions. But if in doing so they contravened the law or 'good practice guidance', their transgression would become a matter for public policy. The prospects of any 'pure' form of communitarian empowerment emerging without such qualifications in our complex, regulated society seems remote. It would therefore be less misleading though less rhetorically attractive for policy makers to use the language of 'shared power' rather than 'empowerment.'

Beyond neighbourhood participation

The continuing importance of national agencies is recognised in the neighbourhood renewal strategy and in SIPs, but the absence at times from neighbourhood partnership meetings of city and national agencies can have a demoralising effect and not all communities are able to make an effective direct link to local or national government agencies. However, evidence from some regeneration experience suggests that neighbourhoods are not necessarily or inevitably the isolated units of low bridging social capital that some writers suggest they might be. Community-based organisations can provide support for the notion that community can be both inwardly strong and outward looking. Groups can use their office and other resources to support networks that connect them to the wider city or region, to engage in public policy debates and to take action in the wider area, city and beyond. These wider city and national contexts for community participation can be as important as the neighbourhood context. Many neighbourhood regeneration initiatives have their origin in a combination of city and national level concern and in national developments such as 'democratic renewal'.

Transforming civic culture

Participation in governance or in activities that touch on governance offers an opportunity to connect residents with external agencies that have a responsibility for their neighbourhood. It therefore addresses one of the crucial weaknesses in the social capital of poorer groups. However, residents of deprived areas undergoing regeneration are in many respects less likely to be active than are residents of other areas. Participation is likely to be confined to a relatively small number of activists and people who are motivated by personal experience, interests or circumstances to seek to influence the governance process. This means that public policy encouraging community involvement is seeking a radical transformation of civic behaviour to overcome the impediments to active citizenship amongst the residents of regeneration areas. Despite the significant levels of resources devoted to consultation and involvement, it is not clear that the scale of the transformation in civic culture that is being sought is fully appreciated by all public officials.

Conclusions: lessons for other policy fields

This section concludes with some key lessons and guidelines for other policy fields. They should be read with two essential arguments for a focus on social relations in public policy in mind. First, the popular conviction that social relations are important means that democratic governance without reference to community is impossible. Secondly, without reference to community, the impact of public policy cannot be judged since the impact depends on the social relations existing in specific places at particular times.

In summary, key lessons for public policy from neighbourhood regeneration are, first, that local political institutions and policies can assist the development of community identity. Second, local political institutions and public policy interact with city, national and wider cultural factors so making it hard to predict how easily community can be built in each place. Third, sustainable models for fostering stronger community identities and community participation can be developed successfully. Seven guidelines for developing community participation in other policy fields can be suggested.

Internal and external factors combine in unpredictable ways

Policy for neighbourhood regeneration has used the concept of community in various ways to inform its approach to improving neighbourhood conditions. Other policy fields could learn that poverty and other symptoms of poor conditions are best seen as the results of external – economic, political and social forces – as well as internal forces, manifested in symptoms of 'community breakdown'. Symptoms of 'community breakdown' – vandalism, crime, incivility, hopelessness, and so on – may nevertheless co-exist with strong internal ties based on family, friendship and voluntary groups and with weak links to the external labour markets, political opportunity structures and other resources of the city and nation. However, social conditions and relations within neighbourhoods cannot be read off from the general social and economic conditions of the region or nation surrounding them nor should these contextual factors be ignored. A complex interaction of contextual and neighbourhood factors creates living environments that are more varied and promising than would be imagined by those who focus only on external forces. It is, though, a mistake to use 'community' as a synonym for residents or neighbourhood. Homogeneity of community identity cannot be assumed either at neighbourhood level or in other settings.

Fostering 'community' can be both an end and a means to other ends

Regeneration policy makers have learned to see building community as a goal in itself and as an agent of change towards other desired goals, in which the residents' as well as policy makers' aspirations have to be reflected. The political and other structures created for regeneration aim to support community development as an end in itself with 'community' valued as a certain type of social relations. Even though it is hard to specify comprehensively what set of relations is desired, a sense of community might be reflected in 'community spirit', reduced stigma and neighbourhood popularity. As a means to an end, a sense of community might be fostered as a way of improving service delivery, increasing individual employability and skills and reducing crime, for example. In some circumstances, residents can become decision-maker and service provider, but this is not essential. Other policy fields would benefit from a similarly catholic analysis of the purposes of community building, with acknowledgement of the aspirations of the people they hope to support into closer relationships with each and with policy makers, on one hand, and, on the other, recognition that low levels of community identity may be the product of wider external factors.

Well-designed structures for participation are necessary but not sufficient

The remedies for some of the disadvantages residents of regeneration areas suffer when asked to participate include the creation of structures that are well designed and resourced. This applies equally in other policy fields. The opportunity structure for participation needs to be permeable enough to facilitate direct action as well as more conventional behaviour. It needs to show that it will allow citizens as well as external agencies to get their concerns onto the agenda of policy-making and achieve results. Opportunity structures for participation are, however, necessary but not sufficient to engender citizen participation. The outcome could be further alienation rather than greater activism if people conclude it is not worthwhile to raise issues that they feel are important because they will not be resolved. People need to feel a sense of efficacy, with residents not necessarily achieving everything they ask for but gaining a perception that they have been listened to and their views taken seriously, otherwise they may give up. Demonstrable progress will also assist their neighbours to see that community activists can be trusted and that participation is worthwhile. Inroads can be made into the structural impediments to participation and one key factor is the progress that residents see with improvements they consider important.

Community participation is hard to achieve and especially hard where it is least apparent

'Community participation' in governance is hard to achieve anywhere, because it involves a transformation of civic behaviour and relationships between neighbours, on one hand, and between residents and public agencies, on the other. It is particularly hard in many regeneration areas because of the socio-economic circumstances that are least propitious for community participation. There may also be impediments such as short timescales for consultation. However, 'top down' efforts by public bodies can have a crucial impact on the creation of mechanisms and structures for participation, especially where conditions for achieving such connections are not propitious. Some studies show that local policies and structures can be developed that achieve inclusion and power sharing for residents' representatives, even in adverse circumstances. In other policy fields, the skewed nature of participation patterns may not be so apparent, requiring attention to the question of who participates and how those who tend to self-exclude can be included.

Community empowerment may be too ambitious – sharing power may be what is wanted

Sometimes the well-meaning call for community empowerment demonstrates a failure to grasp the nature of what such an ambition would mean. Apart from the transformation in civic behaviour implied, the rhetoric suggests a degree of power over services and facilities that is unlikely to apply because of the complexity of contemporary society and the need for regulation and accountability for public funding. Also, the use of community empowerment without recognition of the difficulties of achieving it carries the danger of compounding the alienation many people already feel about how their neighbourhood is governed. At several points, this essay has used the example of community-based housing associations in Scotland to illustrate what can be achieved by a combination of public policy and resident action to build community. This and other models for neighbourhood management generally involve power *sharing* rather than 'control'. But there is a surprising lack of models that create such new balances between residents and public agencies providing services to people at neighbourhood level in other service fields. Education and health services, for example, should be providing more examples of public services that are delivered in partnership; and public action is required to ensure that crucial public services such as privatised bus services are opened up to the influence of users in partnership with funders.

Participation at one level or in one policy field may lead to another

Community participation can be restricted to neighbourhood level, or whatever the immediate focus is in other policy spheres, but doing so is likely to mean not achieving the results wanted by citizens and not addressing the paucity of links from community to wider networks. If the efforts of regeneration professionals to build community are not supported by officials in other policy fields, they are less likely to succeed in reducing the alienation already felt by people whose previous experience leads them to distrust public agencies. This is partly why the policy frameworks for regeneration stress partnership so strongly. Community participation can therefore build bridges to connect people and policymakers within neighbourhoods into wider networks. These vertical links are assisted by the presence of government agencies and other actors to show how they are listening and delivering results and there are also examples of community activists in poor areas developing their own links and the skills necessary to lobby effectively on the national stage. Practitioners in other policy fields will find also that debates about problems faced by their service users will not have the same boundaries for citizens as are imposed by the boundaries of their service or organisation.

Support is needed to foster participation

Activists need support to take part and the large scale public funding of voluntary organisations in many spheres of public policy in the UK shows that this is recognised. The resources required include *sustained* support for voluntary and community groups as well as other resources for training, information and surveys of public opinion to supplement activists' inputs, for example. The corollary of this argument is that public policy that ignores the differences in people's ability to take advantage of participatory arrangements and opportunities is likely to reinforce existing social, political and economic inequality. Community *development* as well as community participation is required. This suggests a need for a careful audit of the impact of public funding by local and national governments for voluntary activity. The impact on different social groups and geographical areas should not disproportionately favour those who are already privileged. Professionals and politicians also need support to develop participation. Some local agencies and professional groups are more experienced and enthusiastic about participation than others and this has meant uneven development. Regeneration and housing professionals are amongst those who have had more experience of building participation policies and structures. Training and development for public officials needs to find new ways of allowing experience to be shared with many more public officials so that they are able to see that helping to foster a sense of community is a skill they can and should acquire.

References

Atkinson R and Kintrea K (2001) 'Disentangling Area Effects: Evidence from Deprived and Non-deprived Neighbourhoods' *Urban Studies* 38:12

Buck N (2001) 'Identifying Neighbourhood Effects on Social Exclusion' *Urban Studies* 38:12

Chanan G, Gilchrist A, and West A (1999) *SRB6: Involving the Community* London: Community Development Foundation

Clapham D and Kintrea K (1992) *Housing Co-operatives in Britain* Harlow: Longman.

Clapham D and Kintrea K (2000) 'Community Based Housing Organisations and the Local Governance Debate' *Housing Studies* 15:4

Clapham D, Kintrea K, Malcolm J, Parkey H and Scott S (1995) *A Baseline Study of Housing Management in Scotland* Scottish Office, Edinburgh: HMSO

Cooke P (ed) (1989) *Localities: The Changing Face of Britain* London: Unwin Hyman

Docherty I, Goodlad R and Paddison R (2001) 'Civic culture, community and citizen participation in contrasting neighbourhoods' *Urban Studies* 38:12

Duncan P and Thomas S (2000) *Neighbourhood Regeneration: Resourcing Community Involvement* Bristol: The Policy Press

Forrest R and Kearns A (1999) *Joined-Up Places: Social cohesion and neighbourhood regeneration* York: York Publishing Services

Forrest R and Kearns A (2001) 'Social Cohesion, Social Capital and the Neighbourhood' *Urban Studies* 38:12

Goodlad R (2000) *From Public to Community Housing? Scottish experiences and prospects* London: Forum on the Future of Social Housing, ippr

Goodlad R (2001) 'Developments in tenant participation: accounting for growth' in *Two Steps Forward: housing policy into the new millennium* Cowan D and Marsh A (eds) Bristol: The Policy Press

Hall P (1999) 'Social Capital in Britain' *British Journal of Political Science* 29:3

Hastings A, McArthur A and McGregor A (1996) *Less than Equal? Community organisations and estate regeneration partnerships* Bristol: The Policy Press

Hoggett P (1997) 'Contested Communities' in Hoggett P (ed) *Contested Communities: Experiences, struggles, policies* Bristol: The Policy Press

Jones C and Murie A (1999) *Reviewing the Right to Buy* Birmingham: University of Birmingham

Katz JE, Rice E and Aspden P (2001) 'The Internet, 1995-2000: Access, Civic Involvement, and Social Interaction' *American Behavioural Scientist* 45:3

Lowndes V, Stoker G, Pratchett L, Leach S and Wingfield M (1998) *Enhancing Public Participation in Local Government* London: Department of the Environment, Transport and the Regions

Maloney WA, Smith G and Stoker G (2001) 'Social Capital and Associational Life' in Baron S, Field J and Schuller T *Social Capital: Critical Perspectives* Oxford: Oxford University Press

Meegan R and Mitchell A (2001) 'It's Not Community Round Here, It's Neighbourhood': Neighbourhood Change and Cohesion in Urban Regeneration Policies' *Urban Studies* 38:12

Parry G, Moyser G and Day N (1992) *Political Participation and Democracy in Britain* Cambridge: Cambridge University Press

Putnam RD (2000) *Bowling Alone: The Collapse and Revival of American Community* New York: Simon and Schuster

Scottish Executive (2000) *Social Justice...a Scotland where everyone matters: annual report 2000* Edinburgh: Scottish Executive

Social Exclusion Unit (1998) *Bringing Britain Together: A National Strategy for Neighbourhood Renewal* London: Social Exclusion Unit, Cabinet Office

Social Exclusion Unit (2001) *New Commitment to Neighbourhood Renewal: National Strategy Action Plan* London: DETR

Taylor M (2000) *Top Down Meets Bottom Up: neighbourhood management* Bristol: The Policy Press

Taylor P, Turok I and Hastings A (2001) 'Competitive bidding in urban regeneration: stimulus or disillusionment for the losers?' *Environment and Planning C: Government and Policy* 19

Turok I and Edge N (1999) *The Jobs Gap in Britain's Cities: Employment Loss and Labour Market Consequences* Bristol: The Policy Press

Wallace M (2001) 'A New Approach to Neighbourhood renewal in England' *Urban Studies* 38:12

5. Community and social exclusion

Marilyn Taylor

This chapter is adapted from the author's book Public Policy in the Community *(Palgrave, forthcoming) and is reproduced here by permission of the publishers. Copyright is retained by the author.*

The language of community

We can learn a great deal about government policy from the language that it promotes. In the 1980s, that language was the language of the market. Those who wanted to get on in any sphere of public life went to business school to learn the language. Everyone got their 'mission statement'; people who continued to suffer poor quality public services became 'customers', and that included people on welfare benefits, who were not in a position to exercise much choice. Public sector services were 'out-sourced'; bureaucracies were 'downsized'; departments became 'cost centres'. The development of a new approach to public management placed 'performance' and 'efficiency' at the top of the agenda.

Some fifteen years later, some of the market language remains, but in the context of a soundtrack that is remarkably different. A new language of 'community' has come to the fore, encompassing a set of ideas which includes communitarianism, 'social capital', community involvement, civil society, empowerment and civic engagement. Thus, at the end of the 1980s, Amitai Etzioni's communitarian manifesto captured the attention of leading politicians and institutions. Shortly afterwards, the idea of 'social capital' was popularised by Robert Putnam attracting the attention of the World Bank which set up an influential Working Group on Participation in the mid 1990s and launched a range of flagship initiatives on participation. At the same time, following the fall of the Berlin Wall, the concept of civil society was celebrated, initially as an alternative to the state, but as the 1990s progressed, also as an alternative to the market.

A number of these ideas have been encapsulated in the formulation of a 'third way' (Giddens 1998) – a path which can avoid both the excessive individualism of the market and the excessive collectivism of the state. The UK government and some of its leading thinkers have also been attracted to ideas of mutuality, drawing on a lengthy but neglected UK tradition. Ironically while many of the traditional mutuals, such as the major building societies are abandoning their mutual status, new forms of mutuality are seen by government to offer the potential to engage socially excluded populations in neighbourhood renewal and to give them a stake in their locality. This is demonstrated in government's growing interest in social enterprise and the social economy.

This new language is also linked with a renewed interest in networks as a way of organising that can either be set against or can supplement the market and bureaucracy. Markets are based on contracts, price and competition and usually associated with business. Bureaucracy is generally associated with government and is based on rules and hierarchies. Networks by contrast are based on trust, shared values and co-operation.

While some see the adoption of this language as mere window-dressing in the face of increasing polarisation and social exclusion, for others it presents genuine windows of opportunity. Indeed the rediscovery of this language is welcome to many who have been critical of the individualism and competitiveness of the market, and the ascendancy of economic over social agendas. After years of market supremacy, it is encouraging to see the attention being paid by policy-makers and academics across the world to the need to invest in 'social capital' as well as the human and financial capital that dominated regeneration agendas in the past. It is encouraging, too, to see recognition being given to the territory between the state and market that tended to be lost in ideological battles between right and left. Increasing attention to social as well as market enterprise offers the potential to bridge the chasm between market definitions of value and the values of those concerned with social justice and social inclusion.

But the very flexibility of this language, which allows it to be adopted across significant political divides, urges caution, as should the frequent and interchangeable use of all the different terms as a 'spray-on' solution to mask social fragmentation and economic decline. 'Community' and the terms that surround it are terms which have been invested with a variety of meanings, depending on the perspectives of the people and institutions that have used them. Several of the terms are contested: civil society is a concept which has changed in meaning over the centuries, while criticism of the concept of 'social capital' and its empirical base has increased over recent years. The overwhelmingly positive spin which accompanies their popular use masks a darker side, which can be divisive and oppressive. With these caveats in mind, Diane Warburton (Warburton 1998) describes community as an 'aspiration', rather than a reality to be discovered, much less returned to. However, if the aspirations attached to this set of ideas are to be realised – especially in tackling the social exclusion and polarisation that characterises our society – then these need to be based on a robust understanding of these concepts and the contradictions and paradoxes within them as well as the promise they hold.

So, what is it that international institutions and national governments seek to achieve by invoking this set of ideas? And what prospect is there that this new language will have more than symbolic value, that it will change the balance of power in society, reduce exclusion and polarisation and/or deliver sustainable improvements in the quality of life of the world's poorest citizens? Can communities, social capital and civil society achieve what states and markets have failed to do?

This chapter considers the ways in which some of these ideas are being used in policy, focusing particularly on concepts of community, social capital and civil society. It explores some of the claims that have been made for these concepts and the criticism directed at them. It then explores their usefulness in addressing issues of social exclusion. It ends by charting the tensions and dilemmas that accompany this language and considering how and whether these tensions can be addressed.

Why community?

As Elizabeth Frazer has pointed out, 'community' is a term that is used both as a description and as a prescription. It is used to describe people who live in the same place or share a common identity. It is also used to describe policies and services directed at 'communities'. But it is also used in a normative way that ascribes certain values and assumptions to people who share a place or an identity.

Focusing for now on the prescriptive or normative use of the term, community and other terms associated with it tend to bring with them the following assumptions:

- A sense of *moral cohesion*

- A sense of *reciprocity* – people being prepared to help each other out

- A sense of *'people like us'*, which implies in turn:
  - a *consensus* of views – politicians and the media will often talk about what 'the community' wants
  - mutual *trust*
  - a sense of *safety* – knowing what to expect of people

As the costs of economic globalisation become more apparent, and neither the state nor the market seem equipped to address the challenges facing society, a focus on 'community' offers an alternative approach to a number of overlapping policy concerns:

- *A rapidly increasing demand for welfare*

  Informal care and support have always been major providers of welfare – financial and social. In some countries, community provision is seen as essential because the state cannot or will not provide. In others, where the state has taken an increasing responsibility for welfare, critics have argued that this leads to dependency and saps people's initiative. There is therefore both an economic and moral need for communities themselves to take responsibility. This leads to a second concern:

- *The breakdown of moral cohesion and responsibility*

  A loss of 'community' is also seen as contributing to insecurity and rising levels of crime and anti-social behaviour. In particular, some argue that dependency on state benefits has sapped personal responsibility and encouraged the rise of an underclass, detached from the morality of mainstream society. Conversely, others argue that the market has produced an individualistic culture, dominated by self-interest. Communities are seen as a means of developing and enforcing shared meanings and moralities in this increasingly individualistic society.

- *The breakdown of democracy and political legitimacy*

  People are becoming more and more politically apathetic. Voting figures are falling in the UK and many other countries, along with trust in the political system. This has encouraged a belief that communities and civil society need to be supported to build 'social capital' and re-engage people with public life. At the same time, governments seek to involve communities more actively through the decentralisation of decision making and implementation and through participatory forms of democracy.

- *Increasing uncertainty*

  In the post-modern world, uncertainty is increasingly seen as a fact of life. Networks of trust, social capital and community are all seen as offering ways to bring some coherence and order to the increasing confusion and instability which many people face.

Community solutions are also sought in other areas: for example, community involvement is seen more and more as crucial to the agenda of *sustainable development*, in the sense both of a sustainable environment and of the generation of sustainable economies. Critics of mainstream economic models are also searching for *alternative economic forms* which combat alienation and exclusion from the production process, while politicians are searching for ways of reviving economies that are in decline from the bottom up through *community-based social enterprise*.

The potential of community

What is it about community that makes it so attractive to policy-makers? This section summarises briefly the ways in which community, social capital and civil society are used by policy makers and in public debate, before looking in more detail at the dilemmas and tensions within them.

Community

It was once suggested that there were 94 meanings of community (Hillery 1955). But Glen (1993) identifies three main ways in which the term 'community' is used:

- Description: community as a group or network of people who share something in common;

- Value: community as a place where solidarity, participation and coherence are found;

- Action: community as an agent acting to maintain or change its circumstances.

These three ways of using the term are often confused. Politicians and policy makers often speak and act as if people who live in the same place or have characteristics in common should automatically have common values, strong ties and mutual trust, and that they will be motivated to act together. Value-based definitions of community emphasise dense overlapping social ties – the only thing that Hillery's definitions could agree on (or at least 69 of them) was that community involves social interaction, area and some ties or bonds in common.

It is these supposed characteristics of 'community' that tend to be contrasted with the impersonality of mass society and the state and also with the fragmented and contractual ties of industrialised society. Such characteristics have been most strongly advanced by the 'communitarian' school, associated with Amitai Etzioni, an approach which emphasises 'respect for others as well as self-respect', responsibilities as well as rights, self-government, and service to others. Based on reciprocity, it is a philosophy that sees the family first and then the community as the site of moral norms and obligations. Driver and Martell (1997) argue that, for governments, communitarianism offers: 'a political vocabulary which eschews market individualism, but not capitalism; and which embraces collective action, but not class or the state'. This is a philosophy which has been enthusiastically endorsed by the Prime Minister:

> The only way to rebuild social order and stability is through strong values, socially shared, inculcated through individuals, family, government and the institutions of civil society.
>
> (Blair 1996, cited in Driver and Martell 1997)

Social capital

There are a number of definitions of social capital. But the concept is most commonly associated with Robert Putnam, who defines social capital as: 'features of social life – networks, norms and trust – that enable participants to act together more effectively to pursue shared objectives' (Putnam 1993). The norms referred to include reciprocity, co-operation and tolerance. Putnam sees these as being produced through 'horizontally ordered' associations, particular those involving face-to-face relations, for example, choral societies and sports clubs. He also links the presence of social capital – built up over centuries – with the capacity for civic engagement which he sees as essential for modern democracy. Peter Hall spells out the significance of Putnam's argument and its attractiveness to policy makers:

> Formal and informal networks constitute a kind of 'social capital', with members more likely to participate in politics and more able to use their social connections to improve their own lives and their community. An organised citizenry can alleviate many social problems and ease the implementation of various kinds of public policy, for instance, by using neighbourhood watch groups to minimise crime. As a result, nations as a whole lose a resource when the ties between individuals erode.
>
> (Hall 1997: 35)

Putnam identified two forms of social capital and his distinction is important to the argument later in this chapter. The first is *bonding social capital*, which refers to ties within communities and groupings – this brings together people who are similar in outlook, interests and education. The second is *bridging social capital* and refers to ties between communities and the external environment – this puts people in contact with each other who are different in outlook, interests, education and social circles. Both are needed.

Civil society

Civil society is a term with a long and distinguished history, and one which has undergone several metamorphoses over the years. In its most recent incarnation, its popularity as a concept has been associated, at least in the North, with the dismantling of the Berlin Wall. As communist regimes tottered and fell, victory was ascribed to civil society, as a counterbalance to the power of the state and as a defence against the infiltration of the state into every area of life. It has been defined as 'all those relationships which involve the voluntary association and participation of individuals acting in their private capacities' (Tester 1992), but in recent discourse and with increasing disenchantment with the market, it has come to be used to describe a way of operating untainted by either state or market. It has also come to be particularly associated with the voluntary, associational, NGO and non-profit sectors in many parts of the world, giving this 'third' sector a much higher profile in public policy.

The limitations of community

While the 'community' discourse has much to offer, it is also one which has been much criticised for its oversimplification of complex ideas, its romanticism and its avoidance of the tensions inherent in these terms. It is to these that I now turn.

First the norms of community, social capital and civil society can have their dark side. The traditional tight knit communities that politicians love are as likely to be oppressive as supportive. Many Victorian models testify to the way that people who went outside the norms of their communities were ostracised and excluded. Abrams (Bulmer 1988) saw the community networks of the past as 'unnatural rather than the normal state of things'. He argued that the reality behind the rhetoric of close-knit working class communities was often characterised by 'chronic deprivation, class consciousness and powerful and extensive kinship attachment' which could be extremely oppressive. Likewise, the norms and networks that prevail on the most beleaguered estates are as likely to be those of gang law and the drugs cartel as those conjured up by the communitarians.

Second, the networks and ties that characterise this language are exclusive as well as inclusive (just think of the implications of the 'old school tie'). The corruption scandals of governments across the globe testify to the negative potential of networks. Community defines 'us' as 'not them'. Indeed it has been said that it is precisely the identification of an abhorrent 'them' which makes 'us' possible. Certainly the value to an individual of the networks and social capital that are associated with 'community' might be increased by their exclusiveness. A relatively closed community is more likely to be able to generate the norms and expectations which generate trust and the sanctions that back up moral norms.

This gives rise to a third tension. Advocates of civil society claim diversity as one of its strengths. But the fact that it contains so many types of group can lead to factionalism. Civil society can be as much a place of conflict and competition as of resolution. And the stronger the values held the greater the dangers of sectarianism, as members of associations and networks discover that their various views of the good society do not match and break instead into acrimonious divisions.

A fourth contradiction within civil society, if it is to be the basis of a genuine third way, is its inequity. Left to itself, argues Michael Walzer (1992), civil society generates radically unequal power relationships. Some critics argue that the benefits of social capital are dependent on the specific social context within which it is created and thus that social capital can work to reproduce and reinforce existing class distinctions and inequalities rather than break them down. In this respect, social capital may resemble any other form of capital, in that those who go into the system with most access to this resource will tend to come out with most.

Fifth, a lot of the debate about community, social capital and civil society ignores politics and power. Foley and Edwards see the centrality given in Putnam's account to small associations, sports clubs and choral societies as simplistic. As they put it:

> We are likely to find that social movement organisations, grassroots interest groups and grassroots political associations of all kinds are more likely to generate Putnam's activated citizenry than the choral societies, bird-watching clubs and bowling leagues he is so fond of citing.
>
> (Foley and Edwards 1996:49)

This relates to a sixth problem – that this language ignores or underplays the role of political institutions in producing and mediating community and social capital. Many of those who promote community and civil society see them as an alternative to the state, while Putnam argues that social capital is in fact the foundation for civic engagement and good governance. But Maloney and his colleagues (2000) provide evidence from their study of voluntary organisations in Birmingham to suggest the reverse, that is, that social capital may be fostered by the state. In their view, governance and social capital interact: the former is not caused by the latter. Community capacity and the voluntary associations that contribute to civil society may themselves be fostered by state investment in the form of community development or grant-aid. It can also be argued that the state, at least in theory, has the capacity to mediate the conflicts and disparities within civil society.

This section has dwelt on some of the tensions within the language of community, social capital and civil society and the network principles on which they are based. But the problems discussed here are by no means inevitable. They are one possible outcome only of the reliance of the network on ties of trust, co-operation and reciprocity in the same way that sclerosis is a possible, but not inevitable, outcome of hierarchy. The weaknesses of this language are simply the flip-side of its strengths and the extent to which the concepts discussed here can offer the potential for positive solutions to exclusion and other problems of today's society will ultimately depend on the context.

If this language is to provide the basis for policies to address social exclusion, therefore, we first have to engage with its complexity. Second, it is important to divorce notions of civil society and social capital from the promotion of any one particular sector. The tendency in many accounts to equate social capital and civil society with the voluntary, NGO or non-profit sector has diminished the explanatory potential of the terms. Third, this language needs to be reworked in terms of its relationship to the state, rather than seen as an alternative. The health of society depends on the optimal relationships between state, civil society and the market rather than the promotion of any one as superior.

Current policy – Community and social exclusion

In earlier publications, I have tracked the different uses of community through successive regeneration and renewal policies (see, for example, Taylor 1998). Major themes which have informed policy over the years are those of community failure, system failure, and economic failure. Thus policies have been developed to re-establish community ties and cohesion in areas fragmented by economic decline or displacement through re-housing; to improve co-ordination between services and agencies; and to bring investment back into declining areas. The 2001 National Strategy for Neighbourhood Renewal seeks to tackle all of these with its emphasis on reviving communities, on joined up action and on jobs. It also seeks to develop leadership and new forms of governance in these areas, which put communities 'at the heart of' neighbourhood renewal.

My concern in this chapter is with community failure and community renewal: the belief that social inclusion means reviving a sense of community in areas which have lost this. In addressing this, I shall first ask whether it is fair to assume that marginalised or excluded areas and neighbourhoods have less 'community', 'social, capital' or cohesion than others. I shall then go on to examine how far popular ideas of 'community' are either achievable in these areas or, indeed, whether they are what excluded communities need. I shall finish by considering how far current policies to revive and involve communities can contribute to social capital and to inclusion.

Is there less 'community' in excluded neighbourhoods?

There is an implication in the notion of 'reviving communities' that neighbourhoods in decline are less organised and integrated than others. This has been disputed. Residents on the estates that David Page studied posed a challenge to the concept of 'social exclusion': their members were mostly well integrated with their local community even if they were not so well connected to mainstream society (Page 2000). Similar findings were reported by Forrest and Kearns (1999).

There is some evidence to suggest that middle class people are more inclined to volunteer and to belong to formal organisations than working class people or people living in disadvantaged neighbourhoods. Thus, Ray Pahl argued in 1970 that, while formal organisations and formal leadership were common in middle-class communities, working class communities were more suspicious of formalisation and the emergence of leaders. Citing earlier research he reported that working class people tended to avoid formality and frequently pointed out that 'theirs was not a "proper" nor a recognised committee'. It is informal mutual activity that is an important source of support in excluded communities, helping to reconstruct and reinforce identity and to create and define 'safe' environments.

Overall, there is simply insufficient research evidence to test hypotheses about levels of activity, informal networks and participation between different types of area, with perhaps the exception of volunteering studies.[2] However, Forrest and Kearns (1999) report a high degree of mutual and voluntary activity in neighbourhoods lacking key economic resources. And there are plenty of case study accounts which testify to high and continuing levels of resident participation and commitment in regeneration and housing programmes in so-called 'deprived' areas over the years. So even if it were true on the broad scale that the most disadvantaged communities were less active and organised than others, there are certainly examples of neighbourhoods where levels of engagement and informal activity have been high and sustained over time. Indeed, the level of resident commitment on the part of residents to many of the neighbourhoods that have been excluded is astonishing, given the difficulties they face.

Barriers to 'community'

There are a number of factors which make it difficult to build community ties in the most excluded neighbourhoods. Perhaps the most obvious is the basic struggle for survival in which many poorer people are engaged. Ralf Dahrendorf (1995) has argued that because poverty and unemployment deny people the opportunities for participation which work and an income provide, they threaten the very fabric of civil society. Forrest and Kearns (1999) report that children are a pivotal element in local networks and women are key actors. But lack of childcare and crèche facilities and the daily grind of having to manage on very limited financial resources inhibit more formal participation. Or as Portes and Landolts (1996) put it: 'There is considerable social capital in ghetto areas, but the assets obtainable through it seldom allow participants to rise above their poverty'.

A second factor is the erosion of the institutional underpinnings of many working class communities. As the workplaces around which many communities grew have gone and with them the social clubs, the chapels and the business for smaller shops and enterprises, local social ties based on work, kinship and leisure have also been unravelled, leaving behind just the shells of buildings and often little access to jobs further afield. Community development trusts and similar organisations have tried to replace this infrastructure through developing economic assets in the neighbourhood, based on community buildings, housing, cultural activities, enterprise development and workspace provision. These are important initiatives, but they need to be placed within an economic development strategy which links these neighbourhoods firmly back into the wider economy.

One of the things that social capital on estates does allow people to do, of course, is to make money on the informal economy: this can be very important for people on low incomes or outside the labour market, but it may lie outside legal limits. The benefit trap and the difficulties it creates for involvement in formal activities or for rewarding participation has been one issue that residents involved in the New Deal for Communities have raised continuously.

A third factor that makes it difficult to build community ties is the high turnover that characterises some neighbourhoods. High turnover in these areas breeds suspicion and accentuates difference. Networks are limited especially for newcomers and they are fragile. As Kearns and Forrest note, in these sorts of neighbourhoods, too many 'people simply pass through on their way from one precarious set of circumstances to another', while those who manage to put their lives together often move on from the most stigmatised and excluded localities (Kearns and Forrest 1999).

Fourthly, exclusion breeds exclusion. I have already argued that communities are as much defined by 'them' as 'us'. It seems almost bizarre to expect communities excluded by the rest of society to be inclusive themselves, especially in a society which celebrates individual choice and advancement so strongly. There can be deep divisions within neighbourhoods, exacerbated on the one hand by the concentration of people with little choice and, on the other by both the reality and the perceptions of rising crime. The community becomes the site of fear rather than security. Identities can be created by exclusion, but the experience of terrorism across the world, of school shootings in North America or survivalist communities there should warn us of the dangers of seeing this as a solution.

Combating exclusion – what sort of social ties are appropriate?

Increasingly, people are asking whether strong community ties are, in fact, the answer to exclusion. Is it really the way most of us live now? What is clear from much of the writing and research on community and neighbourhoods in decline is that the problem is often not the strength of bonding social capital within estates. Such estates can have strong ties. But as Pahl noted, such ties can serve to isolate individuals, cutting them off from wider society rather than linking them to other groups. The social networks of the middle classes on the other hand tend to be looser, less local and more choice-based.[3]

Most people have a variety of communities: through work, leisure interests, residence, through children's friendship networks, even fellow commuters. They have what a number of writers have called 'weak ties' and which provide access to a wider variety of opportunities, including jobs, and to perspectives on issues and problems.

They operate through overlapping communities and we choose which we want to inhabit at any one time. But the reality for many excluded communities is that they have neither the dense overlapping networks of the past nor the sparser overlapping networks required in today's world.

David Page (2000) argues that it is the amount of activity that is centred on the estate (with its own culture) that distinguishes the poor estates he studied from elsewhere. This affects people differentially. The least connected in his study are white younger people who grew up on the estate and who as adults had little or no contact with the labour market. The most connected are older residents who can remember better times on the estate and had maintained contacts elsewhere. Other studies show that ethnic minority residents can be very well connected, tapping into wider ethnic networks across the city.

This concentration of social ties within poor estates is exacerbated by transport and location issues. Many public housing estates in the 1960s to 1980s were built on the peripheries of cities, with poor transport links and few facilities. As council housing was sold off, those with the least choice and fewest networks were increasingly housed together – often, because of allocations policies, away from family and friends. As a result, the more excluded a community is, the less diversity there is within it and the fewer network contacts it is likely to have with the outside world. Some socially excluded communities may have virtually no outside resources of this kind at all. Often this problem is reinforced by the physical design of estates – one way in and one way out, with a bewildering array of closes and cul de sacs inside.

In addition, such neighbourhoods acquire a reputation that maintains exclusion. Post-code discrimination excludes people from jobs and services. Dean and Hastings (2000) report that relationships with family members from other areas become strained because of fear of crime. New relationships are difficult outside the area as people feel they will be judged on the basis of where they live.

The cycle by which neighbourhoods get labelled as deprived or excluded is difficult to reverse when market forces concentrate those without jobs and on low incomes into identifiable areas of social housing. People internalise the label they are given, outsiders reinforce it, those who can leave, and only those who have no choice end up living there. Tenure diversification has been advanced as one solution to this dilemma. But Forrest and Kearns (1999) report that it has had little effect in the neighbourhoods they reviewed and it can set up new divisions.

Policies can inadvertently contribute to stigmatisation by focusing on problems rather than assets and labelling people as excluded or 'deprived'. This label tends to stick and to reinforce rather than resolve problems of exclusion and discrimination. If participation and 'community' are prescribed only to the poor, they will reinforce divisions rather than removing them. Many people question why it is that people in poorer communities have to participate to achieve improvements when the middle classes do not. If community and participation are valuable then surely they should be valuable for all.

If weak ties – an essential currency in today's society – are one thing that is lacking, choice – another essential currency – is another. Two of the most important considerations in choosing where to live are status and safety. There are two main ways in which people could satisfy these requirements. One is to buy into an area where the character of fellow residents is assured by the costs of living there (and buy out again if the area declines). The other is to cultivate one's neighbours. People in excluded communities do not have the first choice and the stereotyping attached to their environment makes it a place where it is not seen as safe to cultivate the neighbours.

In summary, the problems for residents in excluded areas may not lie in the absence of strong community ties and social capital. What they lack is the weaker ties – the bridging social capital – that characterise the lives of most of us today. The 'successful' suburb may have few of the features of community or neighbourliness but will contain people with rich and diverse relational webs. Conversely the poor neighbourhood may have weak and inward-looking networks which nevertheless offer strong support in adversity. Community policies need to focus on the development of weaker ties and bridging social capital. But these should not only depend on jobs. Opportunities need to be created to cement ties across a variety of communities and activities.

Do policies support or damage social capital and community?

How far are policies addressing this issue? Government's neighbourhood renewal policies are based on two years of consultation. They offer an unprecedented opportunity to learn the lessons of the past and to build on the experience of residents and others who have worked in excluded neighbourhoods. But they face a number of challenges.

The first is that communities should not be called upon to manage their own exclusion.

A major factor that contributes to exclusion is the gradual withdrawal of public services, which has contributed greatly to the general impression of isolation, closure and loss. There is simply less local public presence than there used to be. The point has often been made, not least by government itself that professionals simply do not live in these areas (except perhaps the local vicar). Government policy is seeking to tackle the poor quality of services on these estates by bending mainstream spending rather than putting special money into projects, and through the introduction of neighbourhood management. This is an important decision, given that the money allocated to even the most well-endowed area programmes is a tiny proportion of the money spent on mainstream services.

Secondly, it is not only financial pressure that creates problems. Bridging social capital is unlikely to develop between those who live in neighbourhoods that experience social exclusion and demoralised and undervalued staff in the public services on which so many residents depend. These services already have a backlog of under-investment and low morale. The sheer pace of policy change has increased the pressure on many services and contributes to high levels of turnover, which make it difficult to build trust between residents and those who work with them. The growing emphasis on ever more rigorous performance measurement has placed additional demands on workers and the fact that services in these areas are often at the bottom of league tables does not build the enthusiasm that is needed if services are to change. While all these reforms may well produce better services, better outcomes and better relationships with consumers in the long run, the evidence from the ground shows high turnover of staff and considerable pressure. If this is to be avoided, attention needs to be paid not only to the need for change but to the management of change.

Thirdly, while partnership policies have the potential to address some of these issues by sharing resources, knowledge and power, the nature of the partnership process can itself place strain on social capital. Establishing weak ties across the boundaries of neighbourhoods and sharing responsibilities between agencies and communities is the essence of partnership. But several factors could limit the potential of these initiatives. Three of the most pressing are:

- *the lack of time to build trusting relationships*
  This is an issue that is beginning to be addressed in some more recent initiatives, but is equally often placed second to the political imperative to get policy initiatives up and running. There is undoubtedly a need for 'quick wins' to encourage residents as well as to meet political needs, but these must run in parallel with a much longer community development process.

- *the plethora of structural and procedural demands that get in the way of building trust and in some cases seem specifically designed to replace it;*
  Forrest and Kearns (1999) confirm that if residents are involved in very lengthy and bureaucratic decisions, their attendance at meetings drops. My own research suggests that often it is structures and procedures that dominate the early stages of partnership, putting people off before they have had the chance to put their priorities on the agenda.

- *The superstructure of appraisal, monitoring and auditing requirements that excludes many of the community-based organisations who should be benefiting from new policies;*
  Few would dispute the need for proper accountability for the use of public money. But the balance between public accountability and the flexibility and

risk that is required for new solutions to be developed appears to be tipped firmly in favour of the former. This places power in the hands of consultants and auditors rather than the residents themselves.

Fourthly, the current policy emphasis on social entrepreneurs and community leaders pays too little attention to the ways in which they are, and remain, embedded in their communities. There is a danger that community involvement can cut participants off from their wider networks within their neighbourhood. How far it is possible for community representatives to be integrated into new élite networks and at the same time continue their role in their former associational networks? Those who become involved face an incredibly steep learning curve and it is important to understand how the links between them and wider community networks can be maintained and strengthened, if community engagement is to be sustainable. Decision-makers often express concern about the 'usual suspects' and what they see as unrepresentative community leaders. But they also create systems, where only the most determined residents can stay involved, because of the high level of demands and the speed at which programmes need to be implemented. Much more attention needs to be paid to the ways in which community leaders can remain embedded in the communities they represent, what we expect of representatives and how both accountability and succession can be assured.

Fifthly and paradoxically, the money that neighbourhood renewal initiatives bring into communities can be a poisoned chalice. Not only does it bring with it the ever-increasing accountability demands discussed above. But it can raise expectations that are not met and set different parts of local communities into competition, as recent reports into the Oldham, Bradford and Burnley disturbances have noted. The new neighbourhood management policies which focus on bending existing spending may offer more fertile ground for participation, so long as they provide identifiable outcomes for residents.

Finally, there are questions about how far the consensual orientation of the partnership agenda will address issues of difference and conflict. It is important to recognise that conflict is not always negative. Indeed it can be a sign that partnership is working insofar as different parties have the confidence to express difference. Conflict creatively handled can bring a richer, more equal dialogue. But if this is to happen, those working both in and with communities need the skills to bring out the creative potential, to recognise when diversity is essential and when it is counterproductive and to mediate different interests. These skills are still all too rare and even more rarely rewarded.

Implications for policy

I began this chapter by welcoming the new emphasis on 'community' in policy. Although I have spelt out many of the pitfalls of relying on too simplistic or rhetorical an approach to these ideas, any policies to address social exclusion must give due weight to the voice of the people who are excluded and focus attention on rebuilding the links between them and the wider society from which they have been excluded. It must support the networks within these areas which make it possible for people to re-engage, address the forces that exclude people and build the organisational capacity for people to work together to improve the quality of their life. But if the strengths of the community discourse are to be harnessed and its pitfalls minimised, there are a number of points which policy must address:

- *First, policy and practice need to be based in a strong foundation of community and network development.*

  Without this, little else is likely to work. This will involve:
  - building sustainable overlapping networks in communities, of various kinds and offering a variety of 'ways in';
  - encouraging events that make networks visible, reinforce links and give people a sense of common identity;
  - linking local networks into more formal organisations and linking these into outside organisations with resources and power;
  - building the capacity to organise and ensuring that expertise acquired in formal organisations and specific actions flows back into the community at large and is translated into the capacity to respond to further needs and opportunities;
  - ensuring that information flows in and out of networks and that more formal organisations are accountable to the wider community.

- *Policy needs to recognise the significance of weak ties and support the development of multiple overlapping networks that given people choices within and beyond their locality.*

  Although this has received considerable attention over recent years, it is not something that features strongly enough in current government policy towards excluded areas. Many communities will find the lack of transport a real constraint on their mobility and ability to make either strong or weak ties across the boundaries of their locality. Transport came late to the national strategy for neighbourhood renewal, but is now being addressed by the Social Exclusion Unit. Equally important are policies to put excluded neighbourhoods back on the map from which they have disappeared – creating passages in and through these areas, as well as out of them and improving the corridors between them and their surroundings. In this way leaving would not be the only way out.

- *Attention needs to be paid to the development of active policies to reverse negative images and stereotyping and their less tangible causes.*

Dean and Hastings (2000) recommend positive marketing strategies to address this issue. Strategies also need to address the way in which excluded areas are represented in the media and avoid initiatives and processes that focus on the problems of the neighbourhood instead of its strengths.

- *If partnership is to work, connections between communities and their partners need to flow through many passages rather than through bottlenecks.*

This means finding strategies that develop informal links between different stakeholders at all levels as well as formal structures. It means giving people many different ways of engaging in formal structures, through shadowing both community representatives and statutory partners.

- *Attention needs also to be turned to the skills that create dialogue and build bridges between communities and the services they use.*

Capacity building is not just for local residents but is also for decision-makers and service providers. Incentives are needed that will begin to place a higher value on these skills than traditional ways of working. The Audit Commission is currently exploring indicators for community involvement which will need to be put on a par with the other indicators that structure the priorities of decision makers and service providers. These will need to place a premium on community-devised indicators which reflect the reality of community living rather than assumptions based on professional lifestyles and aspirations. Joint training and learning opportunities which bring together communities and professionals will also be important in this respect along with policies that value community knowledge. Residents need to become co-producers alongside professionals in services that are valued and invested in by society at large and not just seen as the last resort for 'the poor'.

- *Policies will require new approaches to risk.*

Network forms of organisation are said to provide the most effective ways of coping with high levels of uncertainty and ambiguity and of generating new solutions to old problems. But the organisational forms which partnerships impose on communities and the regulations which surround their engagement, especially if finance is involved, do not allow for new ways of operating or draw on the potential strengths that more informal processes and relationships can contribute. Indeed, they run the danger of excluding community-based organisations from the opportunity to participate.

●   *Reversing exclusion will require investment in high quality public services.*

Ensuring decent services is a theme of the National Strategy for Neighbourhood Renewal. David Page argues that ideas of neighbourhood management will only work if current tendencies towards economies of scale and 'efficiency' cuts can be reversed (Page 2000). Services are still being cut. While there are clear gains to be made from new approaches to joint working, and new ways of thinking about mainstream budgets, the decline in investment in public services generally has hit those areas most in need of them particularly hard over recent years. This decline needs to be reversed.

I would like to end by stressing two key issues which must underpin 'community' policies.

The first is that we need to understand better how communities work. We need a much deeper knowledge of the reality of community engagement which can overcome both the stereotypes and romanticism to find out how people in communities engage with each other and with the outside world in different political and economic circumstances.

We need a lot more information about the networks that are formed within communities and the importance of both strong and weak ties to those who live there. We need to know about the overlapping networks within communities and what choices people have in making connections both in and outside their communities. We particularly need to know how these networks link with and support community leaders and representatives.

We need more information, too, about how partnership initiatives affect the networks of those involved both within communities and beyond them and how leadership can be firmly embedded within communities. This remains a priority concern both of participants and other partners after years of community development experience.

Some of the research I have drawn on here comes from a rich community studies tradition in the 1960s. This needs to be renewed and extended in order to create a stronger analysis of what value 'community' and its related concepts do and do not add – in all kinds of community. Research is emerging which promises to provide a more robust empirical test of the uses and misuses of social capital, although the rigour with which the concept is approached is variable. Rigorous traditions also need to address the rest of the community language in order to allow a much more realistic approach to the set of ideas which this paper has addressed and a stronger empirical base to inform debate. And we need to develop this knowledge base, not in ivory towers, but through participatory approaches to research.

Finally, it is important always to remember that 'community' is only one part of the solution to exclusion. The strategy for neighbourhood renewal is going forward against a background of increasing polarisation between rich and poor in this country and many others. Excluded communities and their allies are fighting powerful contrary forces. It remains the case that all the efforts of special initiatives can be undone by the loss of a major employer or by world recession and that increasing the incomes of the poor is unlikely to given them much choice, if the incomes of everyone else are increasing faster.

There are some interesting ideas about alternative economies emerging from the neighbourhood renewal stable. It is likely that the initiatives arising out of a successful strategy for neighbourhood renewal will be able to make a considerable difference to some people's lives. It is also important not to underestimate the power of 'globalisation from below', if the strategy does give people in excluded neighbourhoods a meaningful voice. But the fact remains that if we are to achieve the targets set by government, namely that nobody should be disadvantaged because of where they live, the efforts of communities and those who work with them will need to be supplemented on different stages by the efforts of more powerful players in government and at international level. Otherwise, those who do achieve success will only be replaced by others, the positive gains of the strategy will be difficult to sustain, power will not shift and the considerable energy that current strategies are generating will ultimately burn out.

Marilyn Taylor's book Public Policy in the Community *will be published by Palgrave late 2002/early 2003 and available then from all good bookshops or direct from the Palgrave website at www.palgrave.com/home/*

Endnotes

1   Although even in this case there is evidence to suggest that in more affluent areas, imbalances of population mean that there are not enough volunteers to 'go round' in areas where demands for caring are high. Indeed, the costs of housing mean that it is increasingly difficult to recruit a paid workforce for caring and other welfare functions.

2   A study by Fischer (1982) finds that more educated people had larger and more dispersed social networks, while Willmott (1986) cites the 1986 British Crime Survey as showing that, at that time, only 15 per cent of the friends of professional and managerial people lived locally compared to 34 per cent among unskilled people.

References

Bourdieu P (1986) 'The forms of capital' *Handbook of Theory and Research for the Sociology of Education* New York: Greenwood Press

Broady M (1956) 'The organisation of Coronation street parties' *Sociological Review* 4

Bulmer M (1988) *Neighbours: the work of Philip Abrams* Cambridge: Cambridge University Press

Cohen J and Rogers J (1992) 'Secondary associations and democratic governance'. *Politics and Society* 20.4

Dahrendorf R (1995) 'Can we combine economic opportunity with civil society and political liberty?' *The Responsive Community* 5.3

Davies A (2001) 'What is the connection between social capital and volunteering?' Paper presented and the NCVO Annual Research Conference, London, September

Dean J and Hastings A (2000) *Challenging Images: housing estates, stigma and regeneration* Bristol: The Policy Press

Driver S and Martell L (1997) 'Labour's New Communitarianisms' *Critical Social Policy* 17.3

Foley M and Edwards R (1996) 'The paradox of civil society' *Journal of Democracy* 7.3

Forrest R and Kearns A (1999) *Joined-up Places? Social Cohesion and Neighbourhood Regeneration* York: Joseph Rowntree Foundation

Giddens A (1998) *The Third Way: the renewal of social democracy* Cambridge: Polity Press

Glen A (1993) 'Methods and themes in community practice' in Butcher H, Glen A, Henderson P and Smith J (eds) *Community and Public Policy* London: Pluto Press

Granovetter M (1973) 'The strength of weak ties' *American Journal of Sociology* 78.6

Hall P A (1997) 'Social capital: a fragile asset' in Demos *The Wealth and Poverty of Networks: tackling social exclusion* Demos Collection 12

Healey P (1997) *Collaborative Planning: shaping places in fragmented societies* Basingstoke: Macmillan

Hillery G (1955) 'Definitions of Community: Areas of Agreement' *Rural Sociology* 20

Hoggett P (1997) 'Contested communities' in Hoggett P (ed) *Contested Communities: experience, struggles, policies* Bristol: The Policy Press.

Maloney W, Smith G and Stoker G (2000) 'Social capital and urban governance: adding a more contextualised "top-down perspective"' *Political Studies* 48

Pahl R (1970) *Patterns of Urban Life* London: Longman

Plant R (1974) *Community and Ideology: an essay in applied social philosophy* London: Routledge and Kegan Paul

Page D (2000) *Communities in the Balance: the reality of social exclusion on housing estates* York: York Publishing Services.

Portes A and Landolt P (1996) 'The downside of social capital' *The American Prospect* 26

Putnam R (1993) *Making Democracy Work* Princeton, NJ: Princeton University Press

Taylor M (1998) 'Combating the social exclusion of housing estates' *Housing Studies* 13.6

Taylor M (2000) 'Communities in the lead: power, organisational capacity and social capital' *Urban Studies* 37.5-6

Tester K (1992) *Civil Society* London: Routledge

Walzer M (1995) *Toward a Global Civil Society* Providence: Berghahn

Warburton D (1998) *Community and Sustainable Development: participation in the future* London: Earthscan